Interest Groups
and Lobbying

Abraham Holtzman

NORTH CAROLINA STATE UNIVERSITY

The Macmillan Company, New York
Collier–Macmillan Limited, London

144411

TO
JOSHUA, ADAM, AND SETH

First Printing

Library of Congress catalog card number: 66–14204

THE MACMILLAN COMPANY, NEW YORK
COLLIER–MACMILLAN CANADA, LTD., TORONTO, ONTARIO

PRINTED IN THE UNITED STATES OF AMERICA

Preface

Three immensely valuable experiences with lobbyists and legislators have aided me greatly in writing this book. I spent a number of very instructive years studying the Townsend Movement, an old-age pension group. While serving as an American Political Science Association Congressional Fellow for Congressman Richard Bolling and Senator Wayne Morse in 1953–54, I had the opportunity to work closely with and to observe the interaction of legislative actors and lobbyists. A decade later, the Social Science Research Council generously provided me with a grant and a year's free time to study the legislative liaison officers of the executive in Washington, D.C. In the course of this investigation, I interviewed legislators, staff members, "executive lobbyists," and lobbyists for a number of private groups. I wish to acknowledge with gratitude the opportunities afforded me by the APSA and the SSRC as well as to thank all those very busy people in Washington, D.C., who gave so generously of their time and spoke so frankly about their work.

This book would never have been completed but for the understanding and assistance of my department chairman, Dr. Preston W. Edsall. A colleague, Dr. William J. Block, provided me with valuable suggestions regarding agricultural interest groups. Another colleague, Lawton E. Bennett, patiently listened to some of the ideas in this book as they developed and offered helpful suggestions as well as the use of his library. My sincere thanks are also given to Dr. Nelson W. Polsby for encouraging me to undertake this project and for his constructive editing of the manuscript.

This book was undertaken and completed as a result of the encouragement and cooperation of my wife, Sylvia. Each draft had to meet her rigorous standards as editor; in effect, she was an equal co-worker with me in this endeavor. Mrs. R. Cook and Mrs. E. Davis deserve special mention for helping to process the manuscript.

A. H.

Contents

CHAPTER 1

Interest Groups in Society

Chpt I

POLITICAL ACTION by organized interest groups is a fundamental phenomenon of modern democratic societies. Such is the case whether the governmental system is federal or unitary, parliamentary or separation of powers, laissez faire or welfare. In conjunction with political parties, interest groups constitute the principal avenue outside of official public government through which political power is marshaled and applied.

Interest Groups, Dictatorships, and Democratic Systems

There is nothing comparable in dictatorships to that involvement by interest groups in the political process that characterizes democratic systems. Organized groups exist in dictatorships and may flourish, but they are highly circumscribed. They may serve merely as instruments of the state for securing ends which are state determined, or they may become part of the facade of government for legitimatizing decisions. In nontotalitarian dictatorships, groups are permitted to devote themselves to the special interests—economic, social, religious, leisure—of their members. But they are neither encouraged nor permitted to assert their own particular claims in the political world.

Organized groups do, of course, speak out at times in modern dictatorial systems—the Catholic Church in Poland and in Spain, writers' and artists' associations in the Soviet Union, workers' councils in Yugoslavia. Dictatorships differ, and the degree of control they exercise over their societies varies. The Catholic Church in Poland retains its independence and role, in good part, because the Communist Party and its government have felt too weak to attack the church frontally. In Spain, the church has virtually been a partner in the Franco regime. Now that certain ecclesiastical leaders have become critical of this regime, they are able to exert public pressure because the church remains a major, legitimate power bloc and its press lies outside the jurisdiction of the government's censors. In the Soviet Union, on the other hand, those artists and writers who would experiment with new forms and criticize existing practices are subject to the arbitrary control of party and government. At any time, the leaders of the Communist Party may order a "freeze," and the literary associations must fall into line. The state apparatus is available to the party leaders to stifle the avant-garde and reintroduce "orthodoxy."

Private voluntary groups have no independent political role in a dictatorial system. The mobilization and articulation of interests distinct from those of the state, the party, or the leaders are viewed as potentially dangerous. At the most, organized interest groups are tolerated, and all involved remain aware that the limits of freedom may be contracted sharply. A private role may be played by groups whose members share certain common interests, but not an independent public role.

Yet, a close examination into the relationship between interest groups and the state in democracies reveals apparent parallels with dictatorial systems. Democratic governments seek to draw certain interest groups into public administration in order to ensure acceptance and effective implementation of the law. In some cases, interest groups are cloaked with the authority of the state in order to carry out its functions. This is particularly true in the case of medical, legal, and other groups which regulate their own professions in the name of the state and the general welfare. And a number of European democracies have even established special economic councils that complement their parliaments and in which the major economic interest groups are represented.

In these instances, however, either the cooperation of the interest groups is solicited by the government or the groups solicit the government for its assistance or favors. The relationship is more often circular than linear, each endeavoring to court and utilize the other and being utilized in turn. In effect, these interest groups are more or less free agents. They join with the government, criticize it, influence it, or ignore it as such actions coincide with their own advantage or their conception of the common welfare.

What is significant is that in a democracy nongovernmental groups exist, distinct from, and independent of the state, whose separate political role is considered legitimate both within the climate of opinion and by the state. Groups pursuing their goals through politics operate within limits even in democracies, of course. But these limits are basically not state imposed. Rather, they reflect the total political culture and the informal "rules of the game" which vary from one governmental institution to another and which find general sanction in what is considered proper by the rest of society. Where state limitations have been imposed on interest groups, as in the United States, these limitations have on the whole been minimal.

In democracies, interest groups are fellow actors with political parties. The latter are neither appendages nor the highest embodiment of the state such as in modern dictatorships. More often the parties are more powerful than interest groups. Yet, frequently they join in partnership together, and sometimes political parties are even dependent upon certain groups. Particularly in the United States, interest groups may appeal to the general electorate and the populace to override decisions of the government as well as those of the political parties.

In Number Ten of *The Federalist,* James Madison made the point that conflict between groups is axiomatic in society. Where freedom exists, factions will inevitably materialize that will attempt to use government for their own ends. Madison's insight is as valuable today as it was when he sought to influence public opinion in favor of the new Constitution. In a free society, groups will differ, and they will often turn to government to advance or protect their interests.

Government, Private Power, and Interest Groups

Involvement by interest groups in politics, once freedom is acknowledged as a basic condition to group activity, is essentially a function of two overriding factors—the increasing power of government in society and the decreasing power of individuals and groups to secure privately their own objectives. The extent and importance of interest group involvement in the political sphere is, of course, affected by a number of elements: the type of party system, the structure of the government, the nature of the consensus within the country, the general "rules of the game" of politics. While they are influential, these variables have not prevented interest groups from intervening at any and all levels of the decision-making processes of government.

Public government has become so pervasive and powerful that it penetrates almost every facet of one's life—as an individual and as a member of groups. Norms and social behavior involved in television and radio, the fine arts, marriage, sex, drinking, gambling, and the whole area of leisure become increasingly defined and regulated within the political arena. The corporation and the labor union lie within the purview of government, both in terms of their internal operations and functions and in their relationships with the public as well as with each other. What is or is not permissible in these areas can be affected by political conflict as can the specific terms of the rules themselves which emerge from such conflict. This in itself serves as a centripetal force, continuously drawing groups into the political sphere.

With the enactment of the 1964 Civil Rights Act, the national government of the United States assumed, as had some of the states earlier, a positive responsibility for guaranteeing the rights of individuals to fair economic treatment from other individuals and private groups. This constituted a radical expansion of government in the area of civil rights. Public concern over impure air, water pollution, and excessive population, to cite three new areas, extends the jurisdiction of government to the atmosphere, water usage and waste disposal, and sexual practices. National as well as state governments thereby impinge even more intimately upon the social, economic, and scientific spheres within which private citizens and groups operate.

In all democratic societies, government has come to be regarded, although still with some division within the population, as the most useful instrument for dealing with the tremendously complicated problems human beings confront. As modern life has become more and more complex, as interdependence and specialization increase in society, the private power and capacities of any individual or group contract accordingly.(Government is increasingly called upon because individuals or groups cannot themselves cope effectively with their problems.)As interest groups exert sufficient influence to direct governmental powers to their concerns, other groups are stimulated in turn to affect the decisions of government. Groups tend to proliferate with an increase in the complexity and specialization of society and the activities of government. And they tend to merge into larger and more highly organized groups—the better to marshal resources and control strategic decisions.

Organization, "Sine Qua Non" of Politics

An organized interest group may be said to represent a concentration of power. It is a means by which individual units of power may be maximized to exert an impact greater than the sum total of such units acting separately. A group that is organized has, on the whole, a tremendous advantage over comparable unorganized groups. Organization provides a more systematic means for uniting money and effort behind the special functions of leadership. It focuses the energies and political resources of the membership more efficiently behind those interests which they share in common. Without an organization to espouse and advance these interests, individuals within a group may find their voices drowned out by the claims of others. Organization, then, provides a tool for articulating and focusing a group's claims upon society.

The second advantage of organization is that it establishes an accessible source from which politicians, government, and other interest groups may seek support for their own endeavors. For a group not to be organized is to risk imposing upon itself a serious penalty—it has no ready point of access for other groups in society. Furthermore, organized groups can marshal more easily, at the decisive points in the political process, those elements of power which politicians and others consider significant: votes, money, status, public opinion, service, influence.

There exists no one-to-one relationship between organization and group effectiveness. Some organized groups have a much greater affect upon public policy than others. Individuals and informal groups can be more influential at times than organized groups in their communities, particularly as the size of the political community in which they operate contracts. Moreover, unorganized groups of people may exert significant indirect influence upon others and upon public policy simply by being present in the environment. Individual leaders and organized groups, cognizant of the existence of latent groups, may modify their behavior and sometimes their short-range goals in order to placate or avoid arousing such groups. The accepted "rules of the game" may so pervade the world of unorganized as well as organized groups that the latter find they must abide by such rules if they are not to suffer. Nonetheless, when all is said and done, organization in politics remains a *sine qua non* for effective action.

It has become customary in referring to interest groups in the United States to quote de Tocqueville on the point that Americans have a natural propensity to establish and join organized groups.[1] Coming from Europe in the early part of the Nineteenth Century, where the vestigial hold of feudalism was markedly evident, de Tocqueville was impressed with the American democratic spirit. It seemed to him that one of the most significant manifestations of this spirit was the proclivity of Americans to organize into special groups to advance their particular interests. Recent social science research, however, raises serious questions regarding the validity of using de Tocqueville's generalization as a point of departure for examining interest group politics in America.

---

[1] William J. Keefe and Morris S. Ogul, *The American Legislative Process, Congress and the States,* Prentice-Hall, Inc., Englewood Cliffs, N.J., 1964, pp. 298–99; Bertram M. Gross, *The Legislative Struggle, A Study in Social Combat,* McGraw-Hill Book Co., Inc., New York, 1953, p. 19; Alexis de Tocqueville, *Democracy in America,* Richard D. Heffner, ed., The New American Library, New York, 1956, p. 201.

E. E. Schattschneider, for example, notes that the universe of organized interest groups has a definite class bias.[2] Middle and upper income status groups are much more organized; the less providential are much less organized. Survey research data have consistently disclosed that frequency of group membership tends to vary with the status indices of income, occupation, education.[3] In professional households, over one half of the respondents to a 1952 questionnaire on group membership claimed to belong to three or more groups; only five per cent of those in unskilled workers' households maintained this frequency of involvement. Over 40 per cent of those in the latter occupational level reported no membership in any formal or informal group as against only 19 per cent for the professional and 25 per cent for the businessmen households. This is corroborated by data on farm group memberships: wealthier farmers have been better represented both in terms of number and influence than less well-to-do farmers. Furthermore, 41 per cent of the farm households, in 1952, belonged to no group at all. A 1956 Survey Research Center sample showed that 66 per cent of farm households had no member affiliated even with a farm organization.[4] These figures indicate little change has occurred since 1943 when a public opinion survey found over 50 per cent of farmers in the high economic brackets belonged to farm organizations as opposed to nearly 30 per cent in the medium bracket and less than 15 per cent in the lower economic group.[5]

These findings point to the fact that "large areas of the population appear to be wholly outside of the system of private organization."[6] This conclusion appears to coincide also with evidence obtained in measuring participation in public elections: nonparticipants are much more heavily concentrated in lower socio-economic groups.

But the lower classes may be represented in other ways. As against the direct representation of interests—through political interest groups—there stands the concept of "virtual representation." Politicians and political parties often speak for the interests of broad spectrums of people. Many legislators and elected executives hold to

[2] E. E. Schattschneider, *The Semi-Sovereign People,* Holt, Rinehart and Winston, Inc., New York, 1960, pp. 30–36. See also James S. Coleman, *Community Conflict,* The Free Press of Glencoe, Inc., New York, 1957, pp. 21–22.

[3] V. O. Key, Jr., *Public Opinion and American Democracy,* Alfred A. Knopf, Inc., New York, 1961, pp. 502–03.

[4] *Ibid.,* p. 503, fn. 2.

[5] Hadley Cantril, ed., *Public Opinion, 1935–1946,* Princeton University Press, Princeton, N.J., 1951, p. 5.

[6] Schattschneider, *op. cit.,* p. 33.

a concept of representation that extends beyond any specific group. For many, it involves an obligation to articulate and defend the interests of a variety of people within their immediate constituencies. And other elected officials feel a sense of responsibility to constituencies broader than those which elected them. Hence, the interests of the unorganized are not always neglected.

Some interest groups also plead the causes of the poor, the illiterate, the slum dweller, the consumer, the migratory farm worker —to mention the more obvious examples of the unorganized. The AFL-CIO, the National Catholic Welfare Board, and the National Council of Jewish Women push for antipoverty programs, protection for migrant workers, FEPC legislation. So, too, do elements within the bureaucracy of government; they identify with those whom they serve and regulate.

Professional groups that interact with government also play an affirmative role in this respect. Social worker groups, for example, often speak for unwed mothers and dependent children who would otherwise be penalized by those seeking to reduce taxes at their expense or favoring punitive treatment. In August 1964, the National Association of Social Workers protested to the Secretary of the U.S. Department of Health, Education, and Welfare against "midnight raids" on the homes of recipients of public welfare.[7] "Midnight raids" had been conducted by state and city government "fraud squads" to ascertain whether there were men in those houses occupied by families receiving welfare grants provided to fatherless families.

Although "virtual representation" tends somewhat to compensate for the class bias of interest group participation, it is no satisfactory substitute. The unorganized are dependent upon others who have primary concerns of their own. Therefore, intervention by such groups on behalf of the unorganized is unpredictable, haphazard, and uncertain. At any point, the organized group may be forced to compromise in time, effort, and substance. The aspirations of the unorganized are easily sacrificed if the espousal of their interests raises a threat to the internal unity or the advantage of the organized group. And the politician is not only aware that the unorganized tend to participate less frequently in voting and party activity relevant to his own future but also he recognizes their ineptness in exerting pressure upon government.

[7] *New York Times,* August 23, 1964, p. 66.

Organized Groups and Political Action: The Disequilibrium Theory

Why do private groups direct or redirect their attention and energies to public government?[8] One theory, stated in oversimplified terms, postulates that when individuals or existing groups are characterized by stable patterns of interaction—in a state of equilibrium with their environment—they continue to operate and resolve their problems in traditional, private ways. Should the environment become unfavorable and they lose or are seriously threatened with the loss of their established positions, they turn to the public sector of power for assistance.[9]

Recourse may still be had to private action. On the basis of their own resources or in cooperation with other groups, an acceptable position may be reestablished. Business firms may merge, spend more money on research or engage in large-scale public relations campaigns. Consumers and producers may set up cooperatives or private testing organizations. Or individuals may engage in deviant and erratic behavior. But, given the diminishing ability of individuals and groups to protect or advance themselves through their own resources and initiative, purely private alternatives lose their former significance.

The state, on the other hand, possesses a tremendous concentration of power *vis-à-vis* all other elements in society. It represents a great potential which may be tapped. Interest groups resort, therefore, to the power of the state in order to establish a favorable relationship with their environment, to protect or regulate their members, and to restrict their enemies. The state is employed as a reestablishing factor. And as it is introduced into traditionally private or established patterns of relations, other groups are disturbed, and either seek relief in the political sphere or reemphasize their efforts there. Once they are involved, they may find it inexpedient to withdraw.

There is ample evidence to substantiate the general validity of this theory. The classic example is the U.S. Brewers' Association that came into existence as a consequence of a Civil War federal tax on

---

[8] David B. Truman, *The Governmental Process,* Alfred A. Knopf, Inc., New York, 1951, pp. 26–44, Chapter 3, "Groups and Government: Introduction," and Chapter 4, "Group Origins and Political Orientations."

[9] It is an oversimplification to assume that groups turn to government only when their environment has become unfavorable. Government can itself introduce new elements which make it propitious for groups to intervene in order to take advantage of favorable opportunities which government affords them. And groups may see in government an instrument for limiting more effectively those whom they consider their enemies or competitors. Groups may also involve themselves in the political world in order to enhance or strengthen an existing favorable position.

beer. Through its efforts, such taxes were reduced to a minimum. Similarly, farmers in the United States may have been exhorted by Mary E. Lease in the 1890's to "raise less corn and more Hell!"; but they have primarily attempted to resolve the problem of overproduction through the power of government. Their organized groups have supported the adoption and administration of such programs as acreage and production controls and the soil bank. Government has been induced to buy and store surpluses, to distribute surplus food in the schools and to the poor through "stamp" plans, to send surpluses to other nations in the form of foreign aid, and to subsidize the export of certain crops. Faced with a surplus of meat and the prospect of lower prices as a result of overproduction, cattlemen, in 1964, pressured the Congress for import quotas.

Of course, some farmers still resort to "raising Hell" when all else fails and frustration overwhelms them. Witness the recurrent milk strikes and meat strikes. Cattlemen, led by the National Farmers' Organization in early 1964, sought to stop the flow of beef to the market by concerted economic action and by violence. But force is legally a monopoly of the state, which, in most cases, does not tolerate its use by private groups. Moreover, in economic areas, violence is generally ineffectual.

In the noneconomic sector, parents who are concerned about the deterioration of their children's teeth turn increasingly to pro-fluoridation activity. Introducing a protective chemical through the public water system at the general taxpayer's expense is far more effective and less expensive than seeking such protection individually. However, bringing government into the dental health area requires a vigorous organized effort. A variety of groups consistently oppose fluoridation, many of whose members consider this to be a matter of first principle.

Old people, suddenly and harshly disadvantaged by the extended depression of the 1930's, organized old-age pension groups that, for the first time in American history, brought the elderly into politics on the basis of old age alone. The political sphere provided a ready alternative when private means, family, and charity became bankrupt. The adoption of the old-age insurance provisions of the Social Security Act in 1935 represented, in part, a response by President Franklin D. Roosevelt and the Congress to the political activity of the organized aged.[10] Improvements in old-age assistance programs in

[10] Abraham Holtzman, *The Townsend Movement, A Study in Old Age Politics,* Bookman Associates, Inc., New York, 1963, pp. 87–90.

a number of states have also reflected a similar response to old-age pension group politics.

The prohibition movement in the United States exemplifies group politics on the part of individuals who ostensibly suffered no tangible loss—personal or as a group, which is to say that no disequilibrium had occurred. Yet, placed in its historical context, the Anti-Saloon League, which spearheaded the prohibition movement, represented a profound reaction against a violent downgrading of authority of the major elements associated with the League.

The Anti-Saloon League has been characterized as the Protestant Church in politics.[11] Throughout the Nineteenth Century, fundamental Protestantism found itself under increasing attack. A continuing and losing battle was waged by it against the impact of the new sciences, the Scopes trial in Tennessee being merely a minor epilogue. Moreover, a flood of immigration brought into the nation millions of non-Protestants whose native cultures countenanced the use of alcohol. Protestant churches seemed incapable of retaining their dominant position in the expanding urban centers of the country. Rural and small town Protestant America felt threatened by the complex, polygot, "wicked" cities with their immigrant masses.

The Anti-Saloon League represented a major, desperate effort by Protestant leaders to reestablish church authority and power over the individual and society.[12] Alcohol and the saloon were concrete objects that could be attacked as morally indefensible and that represented symbolically those changes in American life which the ministers and their followers clearly found threatening. The Protestant Church could no longer reassert its dominance by itself and on its terms; only through recourse to public government could the individual be saved from the temptation of "demon" rum. Consequently, the League turned to local, state, and national governments to ensure that prohibition would become the law of the land—that the individual would be forced to remain "dry."

Interest Groups and Political Parties

In democracies, interest groups and political parties constitute the major institutions through which individual and group units of power

[11] Peter H. Odegard, *Pressure Politics, The Story of the Anti-Saloon League,* Columbia University Press, New York, 1928, pp. viii–ix, Chapter I, "The Church in Action Against the Saloon."

[12] Joseph R. Gusfield, *Symbolic Crusade, Status Politics and the American Temperance Movement,* University of Illinois Press, Urbana, 1963, pages 6 *ff*.

can be maximized to influence government. Political parties are, as a rule, considered the more legitimate of the two; and they are more intimately tied to the individual, on the one hand, and to the government on the other.

David B. Truman has defined interest groups as those groups (1) having shared attitudes, and (2) making claims upon society. "Political" interest groups, he states, are those that make claims upon or work through government.[13] This definition in itself does not clearly differentiate such groups from political parties. Members of parties also share attitudes and make claims upon other groups and government. But Truman points to a characteristic of interest groups which has value for our purposes: Interest groups use a variety of techniques and operate through any of the institutions of society, not merely government. Interest groups become political only when they endeavor to work through or upon government.

One of the major distinctions between interest groups and parties, then, is the focal points of their attention. Political parties are inevitably concerned with public government in one way or another. Their very purpose is public, and they seek to staff the major policy-making positions in government. Interest groups may be concerned with particular issues and with the staffing of government. On the other hand, they may be totally uninvolved in government and politics. A labor union may make demands upon a corporation which may be resolved around the bargaining table or through a strike. One group has made demands upon another, but neither has necessarily solicited governmental support for its position. Negro leaders may request equal and fair treatment for members of their race from employers or shopkeepers. An agreement may be reached. Or conflict may ensue—perhaps taking the form of peaceful, hymn-singing demonstrations that arouse public sentiment, or of economic boycotts, such as the famous bus strike in Montgomery, Alabama, or, in extreme cases, of anarchic street-rioting, such as occurred in 1964–65 in several northern cities.

Distinct from interest groups, whether they are wholly political or not, parties seek to place candidates on the public ballot under their own labels. Furthermore, the electorate has a voice in deciding which party's candidates will fill public offices. It is only at the local level of government that candidates often compete for public office without party labels. But, even here, party affiliation frequently influences the nomination of candidates and affects the voting be-

[13] Truman, *op. cit.*, pp. 33–37.

havior of the electorate.[14] Elected legislative and executive bodies, moreover, almost invariably organize along party lines and under party leaders—something the interest group may have a hand in, but only indirectly.

The overwhelming majority of interest groups does not seek to place candidates on the ballot. Those relatively few that do, operate through the existing political parties. On the rare occasions when interest groups desire to nominate and elect candidates under the names of their own groups, they must comply with all the legal and political qualifications involved in organizing a political party. But with extremely rare exceptions, such specialized parties in the United States inevitably represent exercises in futility.

In order for political parties to function and place candidates on the public ballot, they must satisfy certain governmental requirements involving public support and organizational structure. They lose their legal status as political parties, therefore forfeiting their right to offer candidates for public office, if they receive an insufficient number of votes in popular elections. Only by securing the requisite number of signatures on a petition from among the electorate can they again compete as parties at election time. No interest group, political or otherwise, has to meet such rigorous legal definitions in order to organize, operate, and influence government.

Parties must always appeal to the general public. Moreover, they are tested periodically in open competition by the acid test of the ballot box. Interest groups may never do so; although by employing the initiative or the referendum, some expose themselves occasionally to the electorate. Parties in the United States, if they are to survive and capture control of the government, cannot afford to be exclusive in membership and must espouse a broad range of policies. Membership in almost all interest groups, on the other hand, is confined to a particularly narrow segment of the population. Ordinarily, only a narrow range of policies concern interest groups, considering the limited number of shared attitudes which their members hold in common. Some interest groups are willing to allocate their political resources to a variety of issues and governmental agencies. But most develop relationships with only a few agencies of government and restrict their policy positions.

[14] J. D. Williams, *The Defeat of Home Rule in Salt Lake City,* Eagleton Institute Cases in Practical Politics, No. 2, McGraw-Hill Book Co., Inc., New York, 1960, pp. 17–18; Marvin A. Harder, *Nonpartisan Election: A Political Illusion?,* Eagleton Institute Cases in Practical Politics, No. 5, McGraw-Hill Book Co., Inc., New York, 1960, pp. 4, 16–18, 21.

The degree to which interest groups interact in politics and with government becomes a significant index of difference between interest groups and parties. In fact, the concept of an interaction differential may be utilized for distinguishing among interest groups themselves.

Wallace S. Sayre and Herbert Kaufman, for example, employed two indices—frequency of political attention to government and scope of political interest—as a basis for distinguishing among nongovernmental groups in New York City politics.[15] Relatively few groups were involved in frequent interaction with the city's government on a broad range of issues. Another set of groups interacted frequently but on a narrow range of issues—health, education, and welfare groups. Many more groups operated in this manner. In a third category were those that had a narrow scope of political interest and a low frequency of interaction with government. These constituted the greatest bulk of nongovernmental groups in New York City. They intervened sporadically, sometimes only once, on a specific issue or governmental decision. The number and population of these groups were in a constant state of flux. Virtually no group was found that exhibited a wide range of interest in public issues, yet intervened at a very low rate of frequency.

The authors of this typology note that any single group in the first category, high involvement and interest, was likely to have more impact upon a larger number of governmental decisions than were the other types. And groups with a high frequency rate of interaction but narrow range of interests were likely to affect more governmental decisions than those that intervened intermittently. Yet the later might be extremely influential when they did involve themselves.

[15] Wallace S. Sayre and Herbert Kaufman, *Governing New York City, Politics in the Metropolis,* Russell Sage Foundation, New York, 1960, pp. 78–80.

CHAPTER 2

Organization:
Strength and Weakness

ORGANIZATION can add to or detract from the unity of the group, its ability to express itself, and its impact upon the political process. The nature of this organization becomes crucial to the functioning and success of the interest group, especially when its size is large, its membership diverse, and its leaders concerned with pursuing a variety of goals.

Organization is more than a structuring of separate roles; it represents a way of relating powers and functions through which the group regulates itself and pursues its objectives. Some individuals are entrusted with authority to make decisions for the group and with specific responsibility for conducting its business. The more ambitious the program of the group, the more its internal government is likely to include a permanent staff in addition to its elected officers. Size, complexity, the nature of the intergroup struggle, all call forth specialization and, therefore, division of labor between members, officers, and staff.

The Active Minority

A characteristic of virtually all organized groups is government through an "active minority."[1] Or, to restate the proposition, almost all organizations tend to be oligarchical. The membership plays a peripheral role in the internal government, whereas a small number of individuals make the decisions and speak for the group. Sometimes they mold the group in their own image. The forms of democracy may be present affording members formal opportunities to participate in policy-making, to vote for their officers, and to compete for office; but the actuality of power permits "insiders" to play a more significant role than the mass of the membership.

Does this characteristic of organization affect the ability of interest groups to lobby and compete successfully with others? What particular advantages to interest groups inhere in their oligarchical organization? Can oligarchy, on the other hand, prove disadvantageous,

[1] David B. Truman, *The Governmental Process,* Alfred A. Knopf, Inc., New York, 1951, pp. 139–55.

contributing to the vulnerability of the group and preventing it from focusing its maximum strength upon its objectives?

The Active Minority Is Functional

There is no doubt that the oligarchic and nondemocratic nature of group organization actually *helps* strengthen interest groups. For a group to accomplish its objectives, its organizational apparatus has to perform essentially representational functions. Its leaders must articulate and often define the positions of the interest group. Carrying out this responsibility requires a considerable degree of competence, expertness, and experience on their part. These attributes contribute to the ability of the leaders to press successfully for the claims of their groups.

In their study of New York City and its politics, Wallace S. Sayre and Herbert Kaufman characterize the Citizens' Union of New York as probably the most influential business group in the city.[2] Its active leadership core includes a small staff of great continuity. The executive committee of its board of directors is essentially a self-perpetuating group that decides all Citizens' Union policies; its chairman selects the chairmen of all standing committees but one. No other nongovernmental group is said to surpass the Citizens' Union in the range of its interest in government or in the frequency of its intervention in the political process. Both of these characteristics are deemed to be products, in part, of *the stability and long experience of its leadership core.*

Many leaders of nongovernmental groups in New York City, the authors note, become intimate parts of the city's machinery for making governmental decisions. Because these leaders have systematically involved themselves in the affairs of government, acquired expert knowledge, developed close relations with the city's officeholders, and possessed influence elsewhere in the political system as well as in their own groups, decision-makers in the officialdom of New York City feel constrained to cooperate with them. In summary, the permanence, expertness, and competitive skills of the active minority have a functional value for interest groups.

Most members of interest groups are either unaware or unconcerned that an active minority controls their internal government as long as results are forthcoming, and recourse to the forms of democracy exist. Leaders generally exercise wide lattitude in determining

[2] Wallace S. Sayre and Herbert Kaufman, *Governing New York City, Politics in the Metropolis,* Russell Sage Foundation, New York, 1960, pp. 497–502.

the positions of their groups, in good part because, in the eyes of the membership, they carry the responsibility for advancing their interests.

In 1942, the CIO's national convention unanimously adopted a resolution for repeal of the Chinese Exclusion Acts. Although this action may have represented a real conviction on the part of the delegates, a student of the politics of the repeal movement suggests that the average worker or delegate "probably knew and cared relatively little about the subject."[3] The leadership had approved the resolution and, therefore, the membership voted to confirm it. The leaders had followed no dictatorial procedure; the floor was always open to objections. It was simply that this practice of ratifying leadership proposals constituted a means by which members expressed confidence in their leadership. In effect, the strategic positions of leaders as proponents and spokesmen for their groups generate consent from the membership, thereby permitting leaders to allocate the political resources of the group to those policy areas which they deem most expedient.

Seymour M. Lipset has suggested that there are at least two additional justifications advanced for oligarchical leadership in voluntary organizations.[4] One stems from the existence of intergroup conflict. The disciplined, expert, and maneuverable qualities of oligarchy enable an organization better to execute its combative role. The group can, as a consequence, compete more effectively with other groups, some of which may oppose it, and all of which may be demanding from government authoritative decisions on policy and procedures. The second justification stems from the composition of the group itself. The very distinctive shared attitudes which characterize its members exclude from its ranks those who hold different or conflicting sets of attitudes or values. These latter individuals may have recourse to other interest groups if they decide to join with like-minded individuals. Therefore, it is contended that no internal structural basis of conflict exists within groups. Internally, groups do not represent disparate elements requiring a "democratic" structure and process to facilitate the representation of competing value patterns and the resolution of basic conflicts. Businessmen belong to business groups, workingmen to labor unions, and farmers to agricultural groups; opponents of the United Nations do not belong to the American Association for the United Nations.

[3] Fred W. Riggs, *Pressures on Congress: A Study of the Repeal of Chinese Exclusion,* King's Crown Press, New York, 1950, p. 73.

[4] Seymour M. Lipset, *Political Man,* Doubleday & Co., Inc., Garden City, N.Y., 1960, pp. 38–39.

That this latter analysis constitutes a gross oversimplification is clear. The AFL-CIO and the American Farm Bureau Federation, to cite only two examples, are broad associations of groups. Their internal politics stem, in large part, from different points of view on policy and the often conflicting self-interests of constituent elements within these federations.

An Active Minority May Prove Dysfunctional

Under certain conditions, leaders may prove to be a source of weakness for their groups. Because of their very strategic positions and the power that they wield within their organizations, they are able to espouse policies that may not correspond with those of the members. Only infrequently do the latter engage in extensive combat with their leaders over policies. However, disclosure of major discrepancies between what leaders say and what members want can be politically debilitating to the groups themselves. Public officials and the leaders of other groups can afford to discount the official position of such groups as misrepresenting the actual opinions of their members. These groups are weakened further by the fact that future statements by their leaders are also subject to doubt. Hence, the very representational role interest groups play can be undermined by the leaders responsible for articulating their interests.

Most groups have some form of communications system through which the membership is reached and group norms and objectives are reinforced. Since the leadership in an organization generally controls the channels of internal communication, it can effectively exclude any criticism of itself. The membership is then precluded from examining alternative points of view in the official publications of the group, and those who aspire to present contrary policies or advance their own ambitions as leaders are at an extreme disadvantage.

A study of labor union constitutions in 1959 revealed that it was the rare American labor union that required its official journal to print opposing views within the group.[5] The study concluded that there seemed to be no sense of need for a democratic information structure within the unions. "In almost all of the unions, the press is under the control of the incumbent administration, so that the official newspaper tends to be monopolized by a few people at the top of the union hierarchy and excludes vigorous controversy or opposition to prevailing administration policies."[6]

[5] Leo Bromwich, *Union Constitutions,* The Fund for the Republic, New York, 1959, pp. 36–37.
[6] *Ibid.,* p. 39.

This practice of self-protection that leaders resort to on the basis of their control over internal communications can, at times, prove dysfunctional for the interest group. It permits the leadership to exclude from consideration by the membership strategic or tactical alternatives to those proposed officially. Such is true in all kinds of interest groups, not merely labor unions.

The official leadership of the American Dental Association, for example, responded in this manner when it was confronted by a strategy proposal at variance with that espoused officially for fluoridation politics. A manuscript on fluoridation politics in Raleigh, North Carolina, which urged proponents to consider the "initiative" campaign approach was rejected by the association's *Journal* on the grounds that it contained commonplace knowledge and that its approach was erroneous. The public health dentists, who have their own association and journal, subsequently published the article.[7] Thereupon, the American Dental Association requested permission to reprint it, indicating that a considerable demand had arisen for the article within the profession. Significantly, in the copy reprinted and distributed by this association, part of one sentence was omitted— that which challenged as fallacious the fluoridation strategy advocated publicly by the association's president.

A number of interest groups provide for the use of referenda among their members. But the leaders play a key role in using referenda and in determining whether they will be employed or not. Their availability generally represents more a bow toward the democratic myth than they constitute a practicable technique for self-government. Referenda are rarely employed because the procedures governing their use tend to be complicated. In addition, individual members are too isolated and dispersed to invoke such action without leadership and organization of their own. In some cases, procedural discretion regarding referenda is left in the hands of the official leadership, thereby placing the latter in a position to affect or block referenda which it considers too dangerous.

In September 1964, a New York physician charged publicly that the AMA had misrepresented the profession regarding social security coverage for its members.[8] Official polls by state medical societies and surveys by the Honest Ballot Association, he noted, demonstrated that a substantial majority of doctors in nineteen states (where more

---

[7] Abraham Holtzman, "Fluoridation: Lessons in Civic Reform," *The Bulletin of the American Association of Public Health Dentists*, Vol. 18, No. 2, June 1958, pp. 2–6.

[8] *New York Times*, September 14, 1964, p. 32.

than 60 per cent of the nation's doctors engaged in private practice) approved of this coverage; only in eight states did polls indicate that the doctors opposed it. Many state medical societies had repeatedly requested the AMA to conduct a national poll on the issue, but the AMA had always rejected their requests. A national poll of the doctors might have produced a clear index of the profession's attitude on social security coverage. Had the results of the poll been favorable to coverage, the official leaders would have been deprived of their monopoly of representation, and serious questions would have been raised as to their reliability. Furthermore, more organized opposition within the AMA might have emerged, and some congressmen might have deviated from that course of action urged upon them by AMA lobbyists.

A third characteristic—irresponsible exploitation of leadership positions— develops at times in organizational bureaucracies, causing intragroup conflict and making the group vulnerable to outside attack. Officers or staff who hold leadership positions for extensive periods may develop proprietary attitudes toward their positions. Sometimes this involves staff supplanting elected officials as the spokesmen for the group.

Dr. Morris Fishbein was at one time considered "Mr. Medicine" in the United States, although he was simply the editor of the AMA's *Journal,* a paid member of the staff. Ostensibly, the president of the AMA spoke for the group and the editor was subordinate to the elected officials. But the latter were elected for yearly terms, whereas this editor's tenure extended over a much longer period. Many in the association felt that Fishbein publicly advocated controversial positions on his own initiative although appearing to speak for organized medicine. As editor, he had kept divergent viewpoints out of the *Journal,* and his strong espousal of certain policies had engendered extensive criticism of the AMA from leaders of other groups.

In June 1949, the annual AMA convention voted to "muzzle" Dr. Fishbein. He was forbidden to speak on all controversial subjects, to hold press conferences except on scientific matters, to publish editorials without prior approval from the executive committee, and even to write his regular column. As explained by the chairman of the AMA's board of trustees, "The membership undoubtedly wishes the elected officials to speak authoritatively on all matters of medical policy."[9]

---

[9] Quoted in Truman, *op. cit.,* p. 175.

Inasmuch as the leaders control the organs of internal communications, possess the membership lists, and act as official spokesmen for the group, other interest groups try, at times, to penetrate this leadership core for their own advantages. The aim of the outside group is doubly served in view of the fact that the leaders speak to the membership in the group's name and ostensibly for their interests. The membership remains unaware that the interests of others are being advanced. Rather, they view whatever is proposed within the frame of reference of their own organization and its representation of their interests.

The American Farm Bureau Federation was once infiltrated in this manner by the leadership of the Asphalt Association.[10] The executive secretary of the AFBF, a nonelected official, was paid by an individual whom the Asphalt Association commissioned to conduct a publicity campaign concerning secondary roads. This campaign was conducted through the publicity channels of the AFBF. Until these facts were revealed by a congressional committee in 1935, the other farm leaders were unaware that their executive secretary was being paid for such services. Threatened at the time by a revolt among its northeastern leaders, the AFBF was considerably damaged by this scandal.

A similar relationship between an agricultural group and a business group occurred in Pennsylvania during a bitter fight between the truckers and the railroads over state legislation. The Grange had a standing interest in the state's road system and no direct connection with the railroads. A public relations firm engaged by the railroads operated through a key leader of the state Grange—its secretary who was editor of its publication. The author of a study of this railroad-truckers' fight points out that the Grange secretary "had great discretion in deciding the legislative issues his organization would support."[11] The railroads hired their public relations firm in 1949; in 1949–51, the annual meetings of the state Grange passed resolutions opposing legislation that the truckers advocated.

In this case, unlike that of the Farm Bureau, the Grange officially endorsed that policy which the business group espoused. But the key position of the secretary-editor afforded the railroad's agents a particularly advantageous access point from which to exert influence to

---

[10] Christiana M. Campbell, *The Farm Bureau and the New Deal,* University of Illinois Press, Urbana, 1962, p. 78.

[11] Andrew Hacker, "Pressure Politics in Pennsylvania: The Truckers *vs.* The Railroads," in Alan F. Westin, ed., *The Uses of Power, 7 Cases in American Politics,* Harcourt, Brace & World, Inc., New York, 1962, p. 339.

involve the farm group in the campaign. Not only did the public relations firm draft Grange publicity attacking the trucker's bill, but also a railroad agent set up his office in the Grange's headquarters and conducted himself as if he were a Grange spokesman. Although the Grange would probably have opposed the truckers anyway, as a result of this tactic by the railroad association's public relations firm, "its anti-truck activities became more energetic and . . . these efforts received wider publicity . . . ."[12]

The Active Minority May Be One or Many

The active minority is not a fixed number; it may range from one individual to a larger number of participants. The National Federation of Independent Businesses, Inc., which represents small businessmen, has since its incorporation in 1947 retained an organizational structure very different from that of the large business groups.[13] One individual established the federation, and he has remained the sole proprietor and president. A public relations division and a full-time lobbyist in the nation's capital comprise the remainder of the leadership. The president is responsible to a ten-man board of directors; but its functions are limited, and he is its permanent chairman. In his hands are concentrated the authority to direct the federation as well as to control its funds.

The California Institute of Social Welfare, to cite an interest group from a totally different area, old-age pension politics, is another example of one-man control.[14] Not inappropriately, its unofficial title is the "McLain Movement." George McLain, its founder, controlled the organization completely. He possessed formal authority to make policy and determine all the activities of the institute. As the executive officer of the CISW, he managed its business. Members of the board of trustees have always been employees of this corporation. As chairman of the board, McLain was invested with the power to appoint and dismiss employees and, therefore, to discharge members of the board. His domination was also based on his personal influence. The members of the group and his staff were personally loyal to and dependent upon him; they considered him to be indispensable to the group. Moreover, McLain's leadership was exclusive

---

[12] *Ibid.*, p. 340.

[13] John H. Bunzel, *The American Small Businessman*, Alfred A. Knopf, Inc., New York, 1962, pp. 69–71.

[14] Frank A. Pinner, Paul Jacobs, and Philip Selznick, *Old Age and Political Behavior, A Case Study*, University of California Press, Berkeley, 1959, Chapter II, "The Spokesman."

in that there were no secondary leaders between himself and the membership.

The U.S. Chamber of Commerce and the National Association of Manufacturers constitute the two largest business groups in the United States. Nominal control of policy in the U.S. Chamber inheres in its annual national convention made up of delegates from the local chambers. A board of directors, however, is the real center of effective control. Numbering about fifty members, it elects the officers of the organization, chooses an executive committee from among its members, and appoints the principal headquarters staff. All proposals submitted for action to the annual conventions are screened by the board, which also controls the organization's finances. It is this board, the active minority, which decides whether or not to hold a referendum on policy issues.

The board of directors of the National Association of Manufacturers, approximately 150 in number, has full authority to effectuate the purposes and policies of the association. The board chooses its chairman and elects the president of the NAM. It also elects the other officers of the association, appoints the standing committees, changes the bylaws, selects the key staff members, and exercises complete control over the budget. In contrast, the annual convention, which chooses two thirds of the members of the board of directors, has only limited policy-making functions.

On the other hand, the International Typographical Union is precluded by constitutional provision and internal political division from establishing a monopoly of power in the existing leadership. There is, in fact, frequent turnover in its leadership. Not only is the official journal of this union required to print opposing views but the justifications for each candidate for national union office must be published with equal campaign space allotted to all. Definite opposition factions exist in the ITU, encouraged and protected by its democratic structure.

To state that organizations are oligarchic or are dominated by active minorities is to oversimplify tremendously. The active minority is frequently not a monolithic entity. Often representatives of different regional, occupational, or ideological subgroups must be reconciled within the leadership. The president of an organization may have experience, know-how, and contacts as well as be respected, and yet he may encounter difficulties in persuading his fellow leaders or his group as a whole to espouse a particular public policy.

The case of the AFBF and reciprocal trade illustrates the pitfalls involved in glib references to oligarchical control by an active minority.[15] In the 1930's, its president and vice-president *were* the Farm Bureau to many people. Decisions were made by the board of directors under the leadership of these two individuals. At the Farm Bureau's annual meeting, the resolutions committee was appointed by the president and dominated by its chairman who was the vice-president.

Despite the position of authority of the president and the influence he wielded, it is noteworthy how carefully he felt constrained to move in reversing traditional Farm Bureau adherence to protective tariffs. In 1929 and 1931, the AFBF had endorsed the Hoover tariff program and called for "higher tariffs on agricultural products." The new president, a southerner and a Democrat, held a forthright position favoring free trade. However, he had to persuade a majority on the board of directors to accept his views. After skillful, patient negotiations on his part, the AFBF's position was transformed, in 1933, into a noncommittal statement on tariff policy. But the Farm Bureau continued to oppose reciprocal trade agreements that did not adequately safeguard the interests of agriculture. In 1934, the president succeeded in drawing his fellow leaders a little closer to supporting reciprocal trade programs. And the following year, the board finally endorsed a policy favorable to such programs. By 1939, he had also persuaded the AFBF convention to propose expanding the Reciprocal Trade Agreements Act. Nevertheless, this resolution was weakened by an escape clause and other "safeguards" to protect agriculture and parity. In testifying before a congressional committee in 1940, the president chose to emphasize the advantages that reciprocal trade treaties afforded farmers—although he had to state the qualifications that the convention had imposed. In lobbying with congressmen, the Farm Bureau president felt himself handicapped by the compromises he was compelled to make in order to retain organizational unity on the issue of foreign trade.

Democratic Norms and Organizational Cohesion

Professor Truman has advanced the theory that the cohesion of a group suffers and the strength of its active minority is threatened, if its members and outside groups judge it to have violated democratic norms. Although, in practice, the internal structure in most voluntary groups is more oligarchical than democratic, it has been argued that groups must *appear* to conform to widely held attitudes regarding

[15] Campbell, *op. cit.,* Chapter IX, "Reconciliation: The Reciprocal Trade Program."

democratic procedures. Democratic norms emphasize written constitutions, the periodic election of officials, free debate, participation
by the membership in policy-making, and the rotation of leadership
in accordance with membership wishes.

There is insufficient evidence to underwrite sweeping assertions
regarding the vulnerability of interest groups should their organization
violate widely held democratic norms. Despite the oligarchical structure of the John Birch Society and the absolutist position of its
leaders, there seems to be no crack in the cohesion of this interest
group of the "radical right." Nor has it lost respectability and legitimacy in the eyes of the general public or the national legislature
because of its organizational structure. Attacks have been launched
against this group by prominent leaders in the Republican Party as
well as by others, but they place little stress on its lack of democratic
organization and spirit. Rather the group is condemned for its views,
its resort to character assassination and communist tactics of boring
from within, its thesis that the end justifies the means. What little
public data there is on the size of the Birch Society indicates that, in
1964–65, its ranks appear to be growing, its cells multiplying. Its
oligarchical organization and the absolute dominance by Robert
Welch have neither impeded the expansion of the Birch Society nor
made it particularly vulnerable.

Labor unions, on the other hand, have been disadvantaged in the
wider political community within which they must operate as a result
of charges that they are dominated by "labor bosses." The closed
and union shop principles are often attacked as repudiating the
democratic concept of free choice. Public and political support for
the Taft-Hartley Act was based, in good part, upon widely held attitudes that unions were not free and democratic and that "labor
bosses" dictated to their members and forced them to join unions
against their will, exploiting them thereafter. Other serious charges
against unions—that they were pro-communist, for example—also
have had considerable impact on public thinking. But the restrictive
legislation on the internal organization of labor unions and on their
economic practices stemmed in large measure from the feelings of
many Americans that the trade union movement had somehow
violated basic American rights and privileges.

The Landrum-Griffin Act of 1959 represented this pattern all over
again. Labor unions were so vulnerable to charges that they had
violated the democratic ethos that their opponents could successfully
push through legislation limiting their relations with employers as

well as with their own members. Although only a few unions were blatantly involved in mismanagement and corruption, all unions were confronted with additional restrictions on their economic bargaining power once labor reform legislation was proposed.

Why should the AFL-CIO, in contrast with the Birch Society, have been so vulnerable to charges of absolutism, irresponsibility, and dictatorship? A number of complex factors are obviously involved. But one that should be emphasized is the low status which unions have been assigned in the United States; they are still marginal groups and suffer from all the disadvantages of such groups. When general suspicion and hostility toward unions extend beyond the upper and middle income strata to include white collar workers as well as some within the blue collar group, it is clear that labor unions in this country have not yet won full acceptance as respectable groups with a legitimate place in society. Marginal, low-status groups are much more vulnerable to outside attacks than are respectable, high-status groups.

\The membership, itself, may become disaffected once this disparity between democratic expectations and oligarchic structure has been publicized; and the group may suffer internal disorganization as well as external condemnation and even isolation.\ The Townsend old-age pension group suffered such consequences as a result of a congressional attack that concentrated upon just this disparity.[16] In November 1935, the Townsendites had scored a startling victory in a special congressional election in Michigan. To many observers of the political scene, it not only appeared that Townsend clubs were making substantial membership inroads in the Midwest and the East but also that their parent corporation, Old Age Revolving Pensions, Ltd., was successfully transforming this expansion into campaign organization and votes. Not only did the Townsend candidate win the Republican primary in a campaign based principally on the Townsend Plan and in which the national pension leaders intervened personally but also he subsequently defeated a Democrat. The final election indicated that voters would cross party lines to support advocates of the Townsend Plan. Furthermore, prominant Republican politicians in Michigan warned that Townsend strength was not confined to this one district, but that it extended throughout the state.

With leaders of the pension group boasting of their plans to enter

[16] Abraham Holtzman, *The Townsend Movement, A Study in Old Age Politics,* Bookman Associates, Inc., New York, 1963, Chapter VII, "Congress Investigates the Townsend Movement."

the 1936 congressional campaign on a massive scale, apprehensive Democratic and Republican legislative leaders united in an effort to thwart such a move. The second session of the Seventy-sixth Congress quickly initiated a special bipartisan investigation of the pension movement. The committee scarcely concerned itself with the merits of the Townsend Plan. Instead, it dug deeply into the internal organization and leadership of the OARP, Ltd. The committee succeeded in splashing across the front pages of the nation's press charges by club members and leaders that Dr. Francis E. Townsend and his partner were autocrats who personally controlled the pension movement and misused it for their own financial advantage. Townsend Club members had apparently believed that they possessed a significant voice in the OARP, Ltd., and that, in fact, the organization belonged to them. In actuality, the corporation was owned and directed by Dr. Townsend and his partner; state managers and regional directors were responsible solely to them, and the clubs had no real voice in the organization.

The investigation succeeded in undermining confidence in the Townsend leadership among the aged, in general, and the club members, in particular. A special pledge of faith was requested by the national leaders, in April, from the 7,000 operating clubs in order to demonstrate that the aged members remained loyal to their leaders. By the end of May, when the final figures were released, pledges had arrived from only 4,450 clubs representing an estimated 1,456,000 members; over one third of the clubs had either dissolved or had refused to express any confidence. Financially the Townsend Movement was severely crippled by the investigation. The quarterly rate of Townsend income, which had risen to $350,000 by the end of 1935, dropped to $180,000 for the first quarter of 1936. The Townsend treasury, which totalled $130,000 at one point during the investigation, had shrunk to $30,000 when it terminated.

As a consequence of the investigation, the Townsend leadership split, and resignations and expulsions occurred on all levels. Entire sections of the Townsend Movement seceded to form rival pension groups which competed thereafter for the support of the old people. And at the Second National Convention of Townsend Clubs, in 1936, the leaders were faced with a revolt that sought to transfer responsibility for leadership to a new set of hands. The investigation so inflamed Dr. Townsend against President Franklin D. Roosevelt that he devoted his energies toward defeating the President, and his pension group was diverted from any concerted campaign in the 1936 congressional elections.

Organizational Types and Organizational Problems

Interest groups may be federal, unitary, or confederate in organization. Each type poses different problems for groups in terms of their ability to marshal maximum strength, shift positions on issues, and avoid or reconcile internal conflicts.

When, in a federation, the elected representatives of the central organization confront powerful constituent units, considerable conflict is likely to emerge. This is especially true when, as in the AFBF, the geographic units tend to reflect diverse agricultural interests. About the Farm Bureau, one student has written: "A 'states-rights' doctrine with regard to its own organization has provided a definite check on the power of the national federation."[17] The national leadership has been decidedly handicapped in trying to achieve a united front in its lobbying before the Congress. During the New Deal period, the California Farm Bureau constantly fought reciprocal trade legislation even after federation officials and the national convention had endorsed it. When production control was the central policy of the AFBF's agricultural program, the Northeast always opposed it. New York's Farm Bureau refused the federation's request that it telegraph congressmen in support of such legislation; Massachusetts warned that if telegrams were sent, they would be in opposition to the bill. And when the AFBF was working through Congress to kill the Farm Security Administration, the Ohio Farm Bureau leaders testified in support of this agency.

Disunity before Congress undermines a national association's claims that it speaks for its own membership as well as its pose that it represents the entire potential group. Legislators are afforded an "out" for adopting any position on a bill since they can assert that those affected by the legislation are themselves divided. If the national organization threatens to marshal its mass membership base against the legislator at the next election, evidence of dissidence within the group reveals the futility of this threat. Moreover, legislators are cognizant of the fact that the local organizational unit is far more significant in their constituencies than is the national organization.

Confederation places a high premium upon the quality of the central leadership and its close cooperation with and understanding of the independent cooperating groups. It is vital that the latter feel that their views are considered and respected because financial support must come from these groups. Leaders of the constituent

---

[17] Campbell, *op. cit.*, p. 20.

groups, who control independent power bases, expect respect and deference from others, including the confederation's central unit. Individuals in the ranks remain members of constituent participating groups, and their loyalty is directed primarily toward these sets of leaders. Their distinctive group goals may, at any time, appear more significant than those of the confederation. A continuous effort to involve the leaders of the cooperating groups in policy and strategy is critical, therefore, to the internal unity of a confederation as well as to its success in mobilizing political influence.

The National Council for a Permanent FEPC was established as a coordinating organization in 1943 by a large number of liberal, Negro, religious, and labor groups.[18] The most important single person in the formation and operation of the National Council was its chairman, Philip A. Randolph. In effect, he was the National Council. Effective authority centered not in the national committee of cooperating organizations but in the chairman and the executive committee. However, Randolph was, by temperment and experience, ill-suited for the leadership of an organization containing widely diverse groups. He was unaccustomed to sharing policy-making and leadership with others.

Failure on the part of the leader of the confederation to share responsibility with top leaders of the NAACP and the CIO alienated these two dynamic groups, themselves at the forefront of the Negro and labor movements. The National Council suffered thereby; contributions from these groups were minimized by Randolph's leadership.

Considerable bad feeling also characterized the relationship between the National Council and the American Jewish Congress, a confederation of Jewish groups, which had participated in the establishment of the Council. The latter "was not always frank and forthright in dealing with the Congress and failed to subordinate personality clashes and differences of opinion as a good coordinating committee must do."[19] The AJC remained outside the main political structure established by the National Council, and the two differed sharply over strategy as well as lobbying tactics. Their failure to cooperate fully resulted in duplication of efforts, confusion among rank and file members, and general injury to the cause.

In order to build an independent base, the National Council sought to establish its own state and city councils. Although these served as

---

[18] Louis C. Kesselman, *The Social Politics of FEPC, A Study in Reform Pressure Movements,* University of North Carolina Press, Chapel Hill, 1948.
[19] *Ibid.,* p. 109.

instruments of the central confederate organization, they were composed of units of the cooperating groups at the local level. As a result, the limitations of confederation imposed themselves all over again. Moreover, some state councils refused to forward money to the National Council until their own fiscal objectives were first realized.

Leaders and Followers: Fashioning a Frame of Reference

Organized interest groups attempt consciously to influence the attitudes and behavior of their members. Since the leaders are, in effect, the guiding force within these groups, they are the ones who play a decisive role in determining attitudes and behavior patterns. Yet this, too, is an oversimplification, for the membership joins or participates in the group because of shared attitudes; organization generally serves to reinforce existing attitudes among individuals. However, the leaders may seek to develop supplementary attitudes so that the frame of reference within which members view themselves, their group, their leaders, and external forces contributes to the commonness within the group and to its distinctiveness from other groups.

In effect, a frame of reference becomes a group reinforcing mechanism. If members operate within the norms of the group and respond to its symbols, the task of leadership is simplified. Leadership policies and decisions will be more readily accepted and carried out. Competitive signals from other groups, organized or unorganized, to which individuals belong can be more effectively blocked and nullified.

Although each group develops its own mechanisms for reinforcing or establishing desirable attitudes, basic similarities are discernible. Most highly organized groups that are national in scope, and many that are state and local, publish their own newspapers, journals, or newsletters. We have noted that one element in the dominant position exercised by the active minority stems from its control over the official media of the group. The larger the size of the group, the more formal and complex its internal communications system. The larger and more affluent groups create many specialized subdivisions, each of which may become a generator of both internal and external communications.

A few groups in the United States have taken advantage of radio and television as a means for communicating with their members. In addition to a twelve-page monthly newspaper sent to each member, the McLain old-age pension group in California invested an important part of its resources in a fifteen-minute daily radio program over twenty-eight stations and, subsequently, also a daily television program. These constituted the principal vehicles for communicating with the members, sustaining morale, and raising funds. McLain's followers were devoted listeners; for many of these old folks it was the high point in their day. Regarding the daily broadcasts by this pension promoter, one team of social scientists concluded: "It offers an opportunity for ritual reaffirmation of loyalty to 'George,' [McLain, the leader] and provides a renewed sense of belonging to something, being cared for, and being in some way a power to be taken into account."[20]

Group identification can be developed by other techniques. Clubs, uniforms, special emblems, and the ritual and pomp of ceremony may be employed. The Townsend and the McLain old-age pension groups sponsored clubs in which their members and, in the case of the Townsendites, the young people, also, could participate. The uniform of an American Legionnaire sets him apart from others and associates him and his group with patriotism. Auxiliary organizations provide another means through which group identity is solidified and group-sponsored attitudes fostered. The American Legion has its Women's Auxiliary to ensure that home and the family do not detract from, but rather contribute to, Legion cohesion.

What specific impact organization and attitude manipulation have upon the membership is difficult to determine exactly. Survey research data demonstrate that members of groups do differ significantly from nonmembers on specific attitude items critical to the groups. Whether individuals who join specific groups have already differentiated themselves in this manner from those who do not belong, or whether the organization, itself, is responsible, is uncertain. Nevertheless, one can assert with some degree of confidence, that organization does have some impact.

The late V. O. Key, Jr., compiled survey research data bearing upon this matter.[21] One question he explored was whether group membership had any differential effect upon political activity. When union and nonunion laborers were examined, skilled workers in both categories responded about the same. Nonskilled union workers, however, evidenced a significantly higher level of participation than unskilled nonmembers. Key concluded that: "Organizations may have their greatest potential to affect political activity, and also the direc-

20 Pinner, *et al., op. cit.*, p. 115.
21 V. O. Key, Jr., *Public Opinion and American Democracy*, Alfred A. Knopf, Inc., New York, 1961, pp. 504–08.

tion of the vote, among those persons not otherwise motivated to political action."[22] The skilled would have voted for reasons other than their being union members; but the least skilled, if left to themselves, might not even have voted. When data on farmers were examined, those who belonged to organized agricultural groups were shown to average higher in their efficacy and degree of political involvement than the nonaffiliated farmers.

Regarding the success of mass organizations in impressing their politics upon members, Key found evidence that the indoctrination of the membership is far from complete. "While the available information does not go deeply into subtleties of the attitudes of members and of comparable non-members, it generally supports the observation that a gap exists between the attitudes of the leadership of mass-membership organizations and those of the rank and file."[23]

Union and nonunion members were queried, in 1952, on their attitudes toward the Taft-Hartley Act. The union leadership had attacked it as a "Slave Labor Act," hostile to labor, and demanded its repeal. How well had the union leadership impressed its position upon union labor? Very poorly, Key concluded. A high percentage was not even concerned with it. On questions relating to the role of the national government in social welfare areas, union members responded more in line with their union leaders than did comparable nonmembers. But the differences were not marked and, as Key pointed out, could be attributable, in part, to factors other than union influences.

Groups other than organized trade unions have difficulty in shaping common attitudes among their members. A *Fortune* Poll of 1936 on whether people believed in the teaching and practice of birth control revealed that 43 per cent of all Catholics answered affirmatively as opposed to 63 per cent for the national sample. Although the influence of the Roman Catholic Church upon its members in this instance was appreciable, it is obvious that a significant proportion of Catholics held attitudes contrary to the official policy of their leaders. Similarly, W. H. Whyte discovered a very strong dissent among members of the NAM to its "free enterprise" campaign of 1950.

We have been citing survey research and other polling data dealing with one or two issues per group. Unquestionably, they do not tap the full range of agreement or disagreement between leaders and members in mass organizations. Key, himself, was careful to qualify his conclusions by admitting that only rough estimates regarding

[22] *Ibid.,* p. 506.
[23] *Ibid.,* p. 509.

the success of mass organizations in conditioning the attitudes of their members are possible on the basis of opinion survey techniques.

There is, however, one carefully conducted study of the differences in attitudes between members and nonmembers of a mass political interest group, and the affect of organization upon such attitudes. The study of the McLain pension movement endeavored to ascertain the attitudes of those recipients of old-age assistance benefits in California who were members of this interest group and those who were not.[24]

Participation in the pension group did produce important changes in attitudes. Members, as distinct from those aged drawing old-age assistance benefits who had not joined the California Institute of Social Welfare, developed greater interest in welfare administration, both in its technicalities and its politics. "Under the impact of Institute propaganda, McLain's followers developed a lively interest in welfare law and administration."[25] Consequently, their world became much more complex, generating feelings of insecurity and a need for protection. Their feelings of distrust were intensified, and the attachment of members to the interest group was also strengthened as a result of these changed feelings and attitudes.

The unorganized pensioner's world proved to be more simple than that of the member's. He felt no strong desire to understand the welfare laws, and his relations with the welfare administration were more easily defined. Nonmembers characterized the pension law as being kind, generous, respectful, efficient. Members described the law in such terms as full of red tape, humiliating, tricky, confused. Fifty-five per cent of the members as against 21 per cent of nonmembers checked only unfavorable items in describing the pension laws; 26 per cent of the members and 61 per cent of the nonmembers checked only favorable terms. The authors of this study concluded that the members' negativism stemmed primarily from their perception of the welfare system rather than from personal unpleasant experiences.

Members were much more prone than nonmembers to designate individuals and groups as enemies or friends. Three of the four items on a given questionnaire that elicited from members the greatest number of "enemy" responses—Chamber of Commerce, a certain state legislator, boards of supervisors—were constant targets of the CISW's propaganda. As members increased their involvement in the

---

[24] Pinner, *et al., op. cit.,* Chapter V, "The Followers"; Appendix II, "The Questionnaires"; Appendix III, "Sampling Procedures and Problems."
[25] *Ibid.,* p. 163.

CISW, these "enemies" were the ones more frequently cited. Again, this attitude pattern was ascribed to perception rather than immediate experience.

The authors of the study are careful to demonstrate that the "perceived enemies" of the members were not entirely of the organization's making. Big business and Chambers of Commerce were unpopular with both members and nonmembers, although almost four times as many members as nonmembers gave "enemy" responses to the first and the ratio was almost three to one for the latter. McLain's propaganda did not seek to reverse the attitudes of his followers; rather it exploited their predispositions and reinforced existing attitudes by making the targets more specific.

The members' attitudes toward their own leader and interest group reflected this official propaganda. Only a few viewed McLain as a "political" leader and the CISW as a "political" group. On the whole, McLain was regarded as a benefactor—shepherd, protector, and friend were the terms to which members responded most frequently. This coincided with the images and attitudes fostered by the CISW through its press and radio media. One result was the imperviousness of the membership to attacks launched against McLain and the CISW by legislators, the governor, much of the press, and many "respectable" interest groups.

Leaders and Followers: Multiple Memberships

A built-in restraint upon the ability of interest group leaders to marshal the energies of their followers arises from the phenomenon of multiple membership. Individuals may actually be members of a number of groups. The family and the political party are obvious ones. It must be recognized that individuals also belong to work groups, religious groups, neighborhood groups, and leisure groups. These need not be formally organized or even have political aspirations, but all make demands upon and order the values and behavior of their members. The family, for example, generally has a greater impact upon the political values and beliefs of an individual than any interest group to which he may belong. Since identification with a political party stems primarily from the family, party ties impose strong claims upon individuals which interest groups oppose with considerable risk to their own internal unity.

The Townsend Movement affords an example of the limits imposed by multiple membership when the leadership of an interest group cuts across the traditional party allegiances of its members. In 1948,

Dr. Townsend sought to ally his pension group with a third party—Henry A. Wallace's Progressive Party. His participation in the National Wallace-for-President Committee aroused an instantaneous and hostile reaction among the Townsend clubs. The doctor felt compelled, therefore, to defend himself in the official Townsend newspaper, denying charges that he had "sold out" the movement to Wallace. Because of this allegation, he complained, the Townsend National Recovery Plan, Inc., had suffered a drastic loss in revenue, which was crippling its operations. Although the Progressive Party's platform praised the Townsend Plan and pledged $100-a-month pensions to all persons over sixty years of age, the closest any national party had come to approximating the Townsend position, Dr. Townsend never carried through his announced intention to support its presidential ticket. For the aged members of the Townsend group, traditional party ties were stronger than their attachment to the interest group and the appeals of its leader.

The frustrations engendered within the national leadership of the AFL-CIO, in the early 1960's, as a result of their failure to swing southern rank and file behind the national position on civil rights, illustrate the conflicts between informal group membership and organized group membership. Many southern trade unionists were also members of that widespread group of southern whites which insisted upon racial segregation.

When the national union leaders sought to rally them behind the national Democratic presidential ticket, a large percentage of the southern AFL-CIO membership resisted on the same segregationist grounds. They responded more in terms of the norms and behavior patterns of this latter group than as union members whose leaders had endorsed civil rights legislation. A *New York Times* correspondent pointed out, in September 1964, that the intensity of anti-Johnson attitudes among southern union members "appears to be related directly to the degree to which Democratic state politicians have divided the membership from the leadership by playing on the racial theme."[26] Even in Louisiana, where the state AFL-CIO had developed one of the most effective political organizations in the South, a poll taken of union members by their national leadership showed that by the end of September, 46 per cent favored Goldwater as against 37 per cent for Johnson and 17 per cent undecided.

An alteration in the extra-group membership of individuals already belonging to an interest group poses a threat to the internal cohesion

[26] *New York Times,* September 29, 1964, p. 31.

and stability of that group. For years, the American Farm Bureau Federation opposed the competition of oleomargarine by resorting to legislation that inhibited its sale in a form palatable to the consumer. A special tax was levied by Congress on the sale of oleo colored to simulate butter. As more and more of its members shifted to crops which could be used in the production of oleomargarine, the Farm Bureau found itself in an increasingly untenable position. The traditional consensus on an oleo policy foundered on the fact that many of its members now had a personal interest in the sale of oleomargarine. Policy statements made by the Farm Bureau against the sale of colored oleomargarine were successively weakened until, in the interests of preserving internal harmony, the group ceased to take any stand on the issue.

In this case, a potentially destructive internal conflict, arising from the transformation of a significant segment of the traditional mass base, induced a prominent agricultural interest group to withdraw from a political position. The alternative was to risk serious and perhaps permanent division within the group. As a consequence of its withdrawal, the political weight was tipped in favor of those groups promoting the use of oleo. In fact, the very division within the Farm Bureau had already undermined the official stance of the national organization; its leaders had been unable to speak for a united group for some time.

In view of multiple membership on the part of individuals, it is questionable whether leaders actually represent their members when they speak in the name of their groups on a multiplicity of issues. When the leaders extend the range of their public positions to those increasingly peripheral to the principal purposes of the groups, the risks to these groups rise accordingly. In 1939, the leaders of the National Grange campaigned within their group and in the Congress against the Townsend Plan, an old-age pension panacea. What were the consequences of their raising an issue completely extraneous to agriculture? They precipitated such hostility on the part of many of their members that they were reported, at one time, to have contemplated action forbidding any discussion of the Townsend Plan in order to avoid disrupting Grange meetings. The leadership had raised an issue that extended well beyond the shared attitudes of the group and cut across those which the farmers held as members of other groups. It should be noted, however, that by controlling the organization, the leaders were in a position to exclude any consideration of the Townsend Plan whatsoever. This action impeded the efforts of the pension leaders who were, at that time, appealing to

Grange locals and to other agricultural groups to communicate to Congress their endorsement of the Townsend bill then being considered in the House.

We can state with confidence that multiple membership is characteristic of individuals in all groups and imposes limitations upon the ability of leaders to guide their groups. Nevertheless, the more involved members are in the affairs of a particular group, and the more they interact with each other and the organization, the more likely they will respond in terms of an organizationally approved frame of reference. Conflict resolution in such individuals, as Pinner's study of the McLain movement indicates, tends to favor the organization.

Diversity Within the Universe of Organized Interest Groups

The universe of interest groups in the United States, and to a lesser extent in other modern democracies, is characterized by a plethora of groups claiming to speak for the same general elements in the population. American labor does not speak with one voice— nor do farmers, businessmen, veterans, Protestants, Catholics, or Jews. Various organized groups, however, presume to speak for them and in their name. Although this diversity has its advantages, it frequently works to the disadvantage of the organized groups involved as well as to the interests of the more general publics whom they profess to represent.

Extreme diversity is a fact of life regardless of the consequences for the groups so represented. The high degree of specialization in the economic world, for example, fosters a multitude of special groups on the part of business, farmers, and labor. Each has more in common that is basic to the economic interests of its members than it may have with the rest of the general group of which it is a part. Businessmen, on the whole, feel an identity with the business community. However, the business community divides into a great variety of specialized trade associations, in addition to the three national general business groups in the United States. Farmers, too, join different commodity groups as well as general agricultural groups.

These special groups rarely presume to speak for the more inclusive group from which their members originate. Rather, they affiliate with larger "peak" associations of groups; or their members also join broad organized groups which represent a much more general set of shared interests and speak for agriculture or business rather than for any segment or subgroup.

Failure to create an association of groups may result in a babble of voices being heard, none of which is really concerned with the interests of the others in the more inclusive group of which they are members. Even if common goals or actions are agreed upon, without a broader organization to integrate and implement decisions, inaction or confusion is often the inevitable consequence.

These disadvantages are clearly illustrated in the Jewish community of the United States, which is itself divided into a large number of organized groups. In February 1964, twenty-four Jewish religious and secular groups participated in a special conference and adopted resolutions calling for the mobilization of Jewish and non-Jewish opinion behind efforts to ameliorate the plight of Jews in the Soviet Union. By October, a leader from one of these groups was protesting bitterly that each of the participants had insisted upon maintaining his own individual position. "The objective of the conference . . . has now almost been forgotten in the shuffle."[27] He urged the 5,500,000 American Jews to persuade their leaders to convene an assembly for the purpose of establishing an over-all body embracing all groups in Jewish life. Such a unified group had existed between 1943 and 1947, but forces for diversity predominated in the end when a number of the groups insisted upon retaining independent positions and acting on their own.

A number of general organized groups endeavor to speak for the major economic sectors of the United States. Business is represented by the U.S. Chamber of Commerce, the National Association of Manufacturers, and the Committee on Economic Development. But small businessmen, regardless of their specialization, have also organized their own general groups. Farmers are represented by general noncommodity groups, such as the American Farm Bureau Federation, the National Farmers' Union, the National Grange, and the National Farmers' Organization. The Cooperative Federation, a "peak" association of cooperatives, also addresses itself to general agricultural problems. Even organized labor is not represented by one association that can legitimately speak for all of the labor force, let alone the union members themselves. The AFL-CIO, the Railroad Brotherhoods, and separate giants, such as the Teamsters and the United Mine Workers, take independent positions on general labor questions and staff their own lobbying units.

In those areas where the major general groups cooperate, the interests of the broader group which they represent tend to be articu-

[27] *New York Times,* October 2, 1964, p. 11.

lated clearly and effectively. The strength each can marshal is cumulative so that a major segment of society seems to press as one for common objectives. Or these groups may devote themselves to different areas of government, ensuring thereby that key centers of power are covered sufficiently and in depth. This works to the advantage of the general shared attitude groups which they claim to represent. Sayre and Kaufman point out how two active organized groups in the New York business community participate advantageously in this manner. The Citizens' Budget Commission concerns itself with "economy and efficiency" in government. Since its primary function is to protect taxpayers' groups in the city against increases in tax bills, it concentrates upon the major expenditure processes of the city government and the officials associated therewith. The Commerce and Industry Association is primarily concerned with the regulations and services of the city government. It interacts systematically, therefore, with another set of public officials.

When the leaders of organized agriculture combined forces, they spoke not only with one voice but with great political influence in Congress. The so-called Farm Bloc[28] represented the coordinated efforts of the Farm Bureau, the Farmers' Union, the National Grange, and some smaller groups in the early 1920's. With wide geographical support and aggressive leadership, the united agricultural community could develop a common legislative program as well as work through a bipartisan bloc of congressmen. But diversity among these groups proved too great to surmount. In the early 1930's, the three major farm groups attempted again to coordinate their efforts behind a common legislative program; differences among them, however, would not permit more than a vague formulation of objectives.

Jealousies among the leaders, competition for farmer support, antagonism engendered by the fact that one group was tied in closer to the Department of Agriculture—all compounded the basic differences that underlay their composition and membership. The Farmers' Union has stressed the family farm, high price supports, the Brannon Plan. It has sought support from organized labor and has worked with trade unions in common legislative projects. The Farm Bureau, the most prosperous and widespread of these farm groups, has campaigned for flexible price supports, reduced government involvement in the production area of agriculture. It has allied itself with the business community, cooperating with the NAM and the Chamber of Commerce in support of "right-to-work" laws and with the Ameri-

[28] Wesley C. McCune, *The Farm Bloc,* Doubleday & Co., Inc., New York, 1943.

can Medical Association in joint opposition to medicare proposals. Whereas the Farmers' Union supported the wheat referendum on production control sponsored by the Kennedy Administration in 1963, the Farm Bureau engaged in an all-out effort to defeat this referendum. The Farm Bureau was closer to the Eisenhower Administration; the Farmers' Union closer to the Kennedy and Johnson administrations.

This sort of in-fighting can prove disastrous if the competitive groups face a united respectable set of opponents. In failing to develop a common position on labor reform legislation proposed in the Congress in 1958–59, the separate labor groups lost the opportunity to prevent the passage of more restrictive anti-union legislation which worked to their common disadvantage.[29] Senators sponsoring reform legislation sympathetic to labor's position found that, whereas the AFL-CIO supported them, the Teamsters and the United Mine Workers opposed all legislation to reform the internal government of unions. When the legislation came to the House of Representatives, the AFL-CIO adopted one strategy and the Teamsters-Mine Workers another. Consequently, the pro-labor congressmen were confused, divided and disorganized; their opponents were united and determined to press their advantage. Labor's disunity resulted in much stronger anti-union legislation than might otherwise have been enacted.

[29] Sar A. Levitan and J. Joseph Loewenberg, "The Politics and Provisions of the Landrum-Griffin Act" in Marten S. Estey, *et al.,* eds., *Regulating Union Government,* Harper and Row Publishers, New York, 1964, pp. 28–64.

CHAPTER 3

Three Democratic Systems: Interest Groups and Lobbying

AN EXAMINATION of lobbying by interest groups in other political systems might profitably precede a consideration of such lobbying in the American context. Our purpose is not to be inclusive, but rather to show how some attributes of lobbying are affected by certain characteristics of these systems. We shall, therefore, compare and contrast strategies and tactics in different countries and try to account for differences in the effectiveness of interest groups.

Interest Groups and Lobbying in Great Britain

Some students of British politics go so far as to assert that British interest groups are "perhaps more massive, organized and effective than the pressure groups of the United States."[1] Whether this is true or not, the lobbying strategies and tactics of British interest groups are shaped by constraining, negative elements within the political system as well as by permissive ones.

A Permissive Cultural Milieu

One of the more favorable elements in the British political system is the culture milieu that approves the articulation of claims by interest groups and the consideration of such claims in the making of public policy. Historically, organized groups have played a traditional role in representing to the state the interests and aspirations of individuals. Not only do groups assume that they have a "right to be consulted" but the Government recognizes this right to be a legitimate one.

In Britain, then, group representation is respected as a germane expression of the interests of individuals concerned with, and affected by, the government. Such an attitude encourages the institutionalization of relations between interest groups and decision-makers. Conse-

---

[1] Harry Eckstein in Samuel H. Beer and Adam B. Ulam, eds., *Patterns of Government: The Major Political Systems of Europe,* 2nd ed., Random House, Inc., New York, 1962, p. 170.

quently, when interest groups lobby—in Parliament with the political parties or within the bureaucracy—their behavior is considered proper, as well as desirable.

The Executive: Center of Power and Primary Focus of Lobbying

A second major point to be stressed is that British interest groups focus primarily upon the executive, not the legislature. The disciplined party and cabinet supremacy are the principal characteristics of Parliament. The political culture reinforces their dominance to the detriment of independent lobbying in the legislature by interest groups. Political leadership in government and party is accorded the highest respect and priority as well as an extraordinarily wide scope of independent action. They are expected to govern rather than to represent; the members in their party are expected to defer to them.

The stability of the British cabinet permits the Government and the majority party to plan and carry out legislation; in effect, to govern with confidence over the long run. The ministers exercise the prerogative of deciding upon legislative policy. Parliament, itself, is not a deliberative body that initiates legislation. It debates, reviews, and criticizes the proposals of the Government. The concept of representation which characterizes the political culture emphasizes Government and party over constituency.

It is, therefore, vital to the interest groups to influence the bureaucratic as well as the politically responsible leaders of the executive in order to have a significant voice in party-Governmental decisions before they are transmitted to Parliament for action. Influencing party and the bureaucracy become important group strategies for promoting their interests with the political leaders of the executive.

Parliament formally decides broad questions of policy but the details and their implementation are within the jurisdiction of the executive. The extensive welfare state in Britain further involves administrative departments deeply in the economy as well as in social services. What the departments do, therefore, is of vital consequence to interest groups in view of the fact that tremendous discretion has been left to the administrators.

As distinct from the legislature, where party and Cabinet rule supreme, the administration needs, desires, and exploits the cooperation of all major interest groups. The broad national consensus on values makes the administrative leadership receptive to claims by interest groups that they have a "right to be consulted." Executives incorporate these groups into the very machinery of government, assigning them positions on the official governmental advisory committees with which they consult. Interest groups so recognized have a direct voice both in the administration of the law and in working out the details of legislation which will be presented to the legislature. J. D. Stewart maintains, in fact, that consultation with the Government provides the most useful key for understanding the relationship between interest groups and the administration, and with Parliament.[2]

Group and bureaucratic leaders interact not only on an institutional basis but on an informal one. S. E. Finer testifies to their close and continuous relations with each other at all levels of the executive.[3] Interest groups need and want cooperation from the bureaucracy and consultation privileges with it; the bureaucracy seeks out these groups to help administer the law and to advise on proposed new legislation. Interest groups, therefore, must have the confidence of the executive departments. If the latter withdraw their trust, the ability of interest group leaders to help their members is seriously handicapped. The bureaucracy is politically secure, moreover, from direct threats by interest groups because it operates under the direction and auspices of the political leaders of the majority party who compose the Cabinet and who dominate the legislature.

For the major interest groups, such participation in the administration of government reduces the attractiveness of strategies directed at Parliament. The privileges and process of consultation with the executive act as an inhibitor upon interest groups lobbying the Parliament. Impressed with the values of consultation, interest group leaders become distrustful of other strategies. Many feel that if they have been in touch with the department, they have probably achieved all that is possible—further pressure in Parliament is not likely to produce anything substantial. Moreover, permanent officials of interest groups are rarely appointed from a political background; rather it is from a professional or administrative one. Consequently, their training and experience militate against active lobbying in the legislature.

Inherent in this distrust of engaging in legislative lobbying is a more significant factor. Interest group leaders are reluctant to jeopardize their good relations with the executive. A lobbying campaign in Parliament could undermine the valuable position that the groups have achieved in the departments. "The more important consultation becomes, the more important it is that nothing be done which would

[2] J. D. Stewart, *British Pressure Groups,* Oxford University Press, London, 1958, Chapter II, "The Process of Consultation," and Chapter III, "Group Strategy."

[3] S. E. Finer, "Interest Groups and the Political Process in Great Britain," in Henry W. Ehrmann, ed., *Interest Groups on Four Continents,* University of Pittsburgh Press, Pittsburgh, 1958, pp. 130–32.

disturb it."[4] The Trade Union Congress, the National Farmers' Union, the British Manufacturers' Association, and the Federation of British Industries, to cite some of the giants among British interest groups, have come to depreciate the value of pressuring Parliament. With the growth of consultation and the close relations with the bureaucracy and the political executive, interest group strategy has, in fact, veered away from Parliament. Furthermore, lobbying in Parliament is much more difficult and less certain than in the departments, for party discipline raises almost impenetrable barriers on important issues of policy, and public relations campaigns from the outside are both expensive and questionable in their effect.

Lobbying in the Legislature

Since public policy is determined by the Government and supported by party-line voting, individual members in the legislature count for little. It is the Government, not the backbenchers,[5] which initiates legislation in Parliament—although some private member bills may be tolerated. The few general committees that exist in the House of Commons have review, study, and criticism functions only. Neither the members who serve on them nor the committees, themselves, are permitted to place their interests and priorities before those of the Government and the majority party. Under such circumstances, the interest group is at a tremendous disadvantage if it attempts to challenge the majority party and the Government in the legislature. Only by exercising the greatest skill in lobbying can groups have more than a routine affect on policy.

Strategy and Tactics in the Legislature

What are the objectives of interest group strategy aimed at Parliament? (1) To secure consideration of the group's claims or the advantages of consultation that the group feels may have been de-

[4] Stewart, *op. cit.,* p. 36.

[5] Backbenchers comprise the great mass of legislators who are not members of the leadership of their parliamentary party. Backbenchers are not hopelessly excluded from any opportunity to exert influence. The Television Act of 1944, which ended the BBC's monopoly and permitted commercial television, represented such an instance of revolt against the Conservative Party by Conservative backbenchers aided by a coalition of outside groups, particularly advertising agencies and radio-television manufacturers. In this case, the backbenchers were assisted also by the Central Office of the Conservative Party. Apparently the Government's small majority in Parliament made it particularly vulnerable to determined back-bench revolts in this period: "There were a whole series of measures, of which commercial television was only one, which were forced upon the Government." H. H. Wilson, *Pressure Group, The Campaign for Commercial Television in England,* Rutgers University Press, New Brunswick, N.J., 1961, p. 102.

nied, overlooked, or inadequately considered. In a limited sense, Parliament is an appeals body wherein a group can attempt to bring indirectly to the ministers for their consideration matters about which the interest group feels vitally concerned. (2) To maneuver between a minister and his party if the Government is not fully committed to a piece of legislation. Professor Finer has pointed out that one successful tactic is to pin the minister between the opposition and his own backbenchers.[6] However, this can boomerang if the minister can maneuver to gain the support of the opposition party in opposing the interest group, or if he can rally the press against the opposition and the interest group. (3) To make the Government reconsider by subjecting its proposals to critical scrutiny. The Government may, as a consequence, feel impelled to alter or withdraw its proposals in response to the criticisms or suggestions engendered within Parliament by lobbying efforts. On rare occasions, Parliament has even coerced the Government into introducing legislation which it had not intended to present. (4) To affect public policy when the decisions are actually left to the judgment of Parliament. On certain issues "free votes" are taken. Since the point of decision on these occasions is the House of Commons, to influence the individual members is to influence the decision. On questions that are considered matters of conscience, the political parties do permit minor defections.

Interest groups have available to them a number of strategies for lobbying in Parliament. These range from what may be called "discreet lobbying" to active campaigns for mobilizing public opinion and mass lobbying by the group's members and leaders with the M.P.s. Formal limitations imposed by Parliament and reinforced by the political culture together with party discipline exclude other strategies as unacceptable.

(A) LEGISLATIVE PARTIES   An interest group may establish contact with both political parties or with the majority party. Sometimes this involves sponsoring an "all party" bloc of supporters. This tactic attempts to involve the backbenchers from both major parties in joint action with the interest group. These sympathetic legislators may send deputations to the ministries, raise parliamentary inquiries, "table" (raise) desirable amendments in the standing committees of Parliament. The relationship between M.P.s and parliamentary party blocs is informal. Interest groups generally encounter little difficulty in persuading M.P.s to serve since the latter merely agree to cooperate with the group, if possible. Participation in these common endeavors can rebound to the advantage of the legislators, for they need to be

[6] Finer, *op. cit.*, p. 136.

informed about the details of legislation and do not have the staff for this purpose. Whereas the party can furnish some aid, interest groups are prepared to provide the detailed information and assistance. This is of great value to the backbenchers because it permits them to acquire the knowledge and skill with which to speak authoritatively on issues. Hence, the relationship is reciprocal; it works to the advantage of both M.P. and interest group.

Political parties have their own functional groups in the legislature to which interest groups may appeal for a hearing. The National Farmers' Union, for example, has attempted to exert influence by presenting its case before the Agriculture Committee of the Conservative Party and its parallel in the Labor Party. If these committees, which generally contain all those in the legislative party who are interested in an issue, are converted to the point of view of the interest group, the influence of the latter in consultation has been magnified. The party committee then provides the interest group with a foothold in the House and in the party which can prove very useful.

Parliamentary amendments are recognized and accepted by the Government as a means for inducing consultation with interest groups through "subdued pressure." To press too far would be to challenge the Government, a step that an interest group can ill afford. Hence, groups do not normally anticipate having their amendments carried against the Government. The fact that a member "tables" (raises) one of their amendments in a standing committee merely makes certain that the group's proposal will at least be examined by the Government. Thus, the issues that concern an interest group are raised through a tactic recognized as legitimate by the ministers. A ministry will, in fact, occasionally solicit a group to propose an amendment in order to secure a test of feeling.

(B) PARLIAMENTARY AGENTS   A number of interest groups employ a specialist in parliamentary affairs from outside the ranks of Parliament. Although these parliamentary agents approximate the American type of professional lobbyist, their functions are more limited, and their roles more circumscribed. Principally, they prepare and promote or oppose private bills which deal with special local situations. The treatment of private bills is primarily nonpartisan in character, and it is considered improper for parliamentary agents to engage in large-scale lobbying in Parliament. But many, of course, advise on all sorts of legislation and are alert to the concerns of their interest groups in Parliament.

(C) DIRECT REPRESENTATION IN PARLIAMENT   Interest groups may seek direct representation in Parliament. Some appoint legislators to their boards of directors. A number have "sponsored" candidates of their own within the ranks of the political parties.[7] That is, the interest group pays a percentage of a candidate's campaign expenditures and continues to provide him with a salary while he serves in Parliament. This places an agent of the interest group directly in the House of Commons, with inside access to the legislative process and party caucuses. "Sponsored" legislators facilitate group efforts to raise questions and present amendments in committees, afford groups an opportunity to have their positions articulated in the development of parliamentary opinion, and advise their groups on political matters.

The "sponsoring" of candidates is considered proper and legitimate although most groups do not resort to this practice. The Labor Party recognizes, and even regulates, the terms of "sponsorship." Trade unions affiliated with the Labor Party are the principal groups to employ this tactic; for many years, it was their sole means for securing representation in the Commons. The National Farmers' Union, *the* organized interest group of farmers in Britain, actively engaged in this tactic in the 1930's but abandoned it on the ground that it might limit the group in Commons more than it might help. The National Union of Teachers is probably the only other major group to emphasize "sponsored" candidates. It has tried scrupulously to be nonpartisan, sponsoring Conservative as well as Labor M.P.s. Its candidates were required to be members of the NTU for seven preceding years and to agree to assist the group in parliamentary matters whenever possible within the boundaries of party privilege.

A satisfactory relationship between an interest group and its "sponsored" candidates can exist only within the framework of the party system and in accordance with generally accepted rules of propriety. The "sponsored" candidate is not the mere instrument of the interest group, to vote and act as it wishes. Despite the fact that the group may pay a major share of his campaign funds and provide him with an allowance, the M.P. owes allegiance to his party first, to his constituency second, and then to the interest group. He will do his best to advance the group's proposals, but these considerations may be overridden by other factors, principally his loyalty to his party and the discipline it exerts.

If a group violates these basic understandings, it imperils its relationship with its M.P.s. Confronted with a conflict between the position of his "sponsoring" group and that of his political party, the M.P. sides inevitably with the latter. Members have resigned from

[7] Stewart, *op. cit.*, pp. 165–201.

their interest groups as well as from "sponsored" relationships with them when they concluded that these groups were insisting that they adhere to the position, claims, and guidance of the groups over those of their political parties.

Formal limits upon the types of pressures which interest groups can bring to bear upon members are also part of the "rules of the game" within the legislature. It is considered a breach of privilege, punishable by the House of Commons, for an interest group to exert improper influence upon legislators. "Improper" includes within its boundaries not merely bribery but also attempts to exert influence through threats, rewards, or punishments and by withholding or granting positions, privileges, and support. To foreclose the possibility of secret alliances between members and interest groups, it is customary in Commons for a member to disclose publicly his interest in any matter in which he is financially involved. Many members acknowledge their connections with interest groups in this manner. More frequently, members may state that they speak officially for some group although no declaration of financial interest is involved.

(D) USE OF INDIRECT LOBBYING TECHNIQUES   Mass pressure campaigns directed at influencing Parliament have apparently declined in importance for interest groups. Stewart attributes this modification in group strategy to the tremendous expansion of consultation between the executive and the groups.[8] The fact that interest groups are welcome in the executive departments is one among a number of reasons cited by Finer in explaining why public campaigns are not as important in Britain as in the United States.[9] The rigid limitations imposed by law upon campaign expenditures and the strict observance of the law also inhibit recourse to this strategy. So, too, do prohibitions against politics by interest groups over television and radio.

Some interest groups do resort, however, to massive lobbying and public relations campaigns. Not all groups are afforded the consultation by the Government that they deem necessary, and some do not attain the respectability and legitimacy in the eyes of the executives that entitle them to intimate, cooperative relationships. Members in some groups may place a greater value than their leaders on lobbying M.P.s and organizing mass demonstrations. Moreover, the Government may make adjustments in response to public opinion. If significant discontent is generated, it can introduce into the Govern-

---

[8] Stewart, *op. cit.,* Chapter III, "Group Strategy."
[9] Finer, *op. cit.,* p. 137.

ment's calculations new political elements which may compel the Government to reconsider its proposal.

Confronted with the National Health Service Bill in 1948, the British Dental Association relied originally upon this type of strategy. At the time, the association had not established close relations with the ministry concerned and it felt that it had not been adequately consulted. As a result, it decided to initiate an active lobbying campaign which it conducted in collaboration with an associated dental group. Subcommittees for lobbying were appointed to meet with members of the standing committee in Commons considering the bill in an effort to obtain their support for the association's amendments. The two dental groups also undertook to mobilize the personal influence its dentists had with these particular M.P.s. A public relations committee was set up to encourage the dentists to enlist the support of their patients in the campaign. In the end, however, this strategy proved futile. The dentists were compelled to fall back upon the traditional device of having a parliamentary agent draft amendments, only some of which a dental Labor Party member accepted as the basis for a meeting with the minister. This M.P. refused to push the amendments to a vote, and the dissatisfied lobbying committee of this particular association had no alternative but to accept the assurances he had obtained from the minister regarding an interpretation of the bill.

On the other hand, the National Union of Teachers, in 1953–54, engaged in a campaign to oppose a retirement bill that would have increased financial contributions from teachers. Its local associations were activated to contact their M.P.s; and each sent, at the union's expense, a number of representatives to lobby in London. The primary purpose of the campaign was to arrange for support among Conservative M.P.s, and the influence of Conservative backbenchers was such that the bill was withdrawn. Subsequently, a similar bill with some concessions toward the teacher's position was passed, in 1955, despite vigorous opposition by their association.

A successful campaign to induce the Labor Government to reverse its decision to nationalize the sugar manufacturing and refining industry was conducted by the largest sugar refining firm in Britain and its special public relations associate, Aims of Industry, in 1949.[10] They endeavored to create a public opinion in the country hostile to the Government's plan. To this end, they mobilized the stockholders

---

[10] H. H. Wilson, "Techniques of Pressure—Anti Nationalization Propaganda in Britain," *Public Opinion Quarterly,* Vol. 15, No. 2, Summer, 1951, pp. 225–242.

as well as the customers of this firm, the employees of the entire industry, and thousands of retail shopkeepers. The latter were particularly valuable allies, for they talked with the housewives who came to shop, and they distributed millions of leaflets as well as ration book holders containing anti-nationalization propaganda. In addition, millions of sugar packages were distributed on which were printed the ubiquitous "Mr. Cube," a clever sugar-cube carton character, and his catchy slogans against the nationalization of sugar.

By November 1950, public opinion polls indicated that over 50 per cent of the people disapproved of the Government's proposal and only 25 per cent approved. In fact many Socialists were themselves not convinced that the sugar manufacturing and refining industry should be nationalized at that time. The campaign succeeded, moreover, because opponents of nationalization were able to take advantage of widespread discontent arising from such irritants as a housing shortage, a cut in the meat supply, a rising cost of living, and foreign affairs problems. Nevertheless, the nationalization of the sugar industry would have probably proceeded without any difficulty if it had not been for the campaign by the sugar firm and its allies. Regarding such a massive public relations campaign, one student of British politics concluded that "it can produce difficulties, make impossible a program dependent upon popular support, and serve to intimidate the Government."[11]

The Political Party and the Electorate

When either party is in power, it consults more systematically with its allies—the Labor Party with trade-union cooperative groups, the Conservative Party with business and agricultural groups. However, a broad consensus on major policy issues exists in the body politic. To win a general election, parties must reflect this consensus. They cannot be too closely identified in the public's mind with the aspirations and organizations of any group. And party leaders, when they come to power, must deal equitably with all the major interest groups; it is expected of them.

The party organization dominates the selection of candidates as well as their election. In election campaigns, the party helps protect its candidates from interest groups by compelling its candidates to say "no" to groups and by preventing interest groups from gaining electoral strength. Even if candidates have signed pledges with interest groups, the dictates of the party will determine the position its candi-

[11] *Ibid.,* p. 242.

dates take on issues and how they subsequently will vote in the legis-lature. Moreover, interest groups are severely restricted if they wish to contribute significantly to the campaign of any candidate. Very stringent laws regulate campaign expenditures. They attempt to deny to all organized groups, except political parties, the right to incur expenses in promoting or defeating the election of any candidate. This has had a restraining effect upon interest group involvement in election activities.

Interest Groups in Italian Politics[12]

A brief examination of interest groups in a sharply divided political system with a somewhat more independent legislature than in Great Britain may serve as a transition to the American System.

A Fragmented Political Culture

Italian society is highly fragmented, characterized by extreme class conflict and ideological differences. No basic consensus unites the major groups in the population. The two strongest groups are the organized Catholic groups associated with the Christian Democratic Party and the leftists and labor groups which identify with the Com-munist and socialist parties. Both are divisive elements in the social system, and their conflict permeates all aspects of society. Not only are political, economic, and social groups split along ideological lines but also the country itself is divided into two distinct cultures, North and South. Political socialization has failed to provide many Italians with a common identity and allegiance; the loyalty of a large pro-portion of them is still primarily addressed to family, kinship group, and neighborhood and village, especially in the South.

As a consequence, interest groups are also fragmented and highly ideological. Political and social communications between interest groups is minimal. This intensifies the division in the country, for the dominant political parties and the groups associated with them cannot even concede the existence of a loyal opposition. In the legislature and the executive, those elements which control the government evi-dence a suspicious, hostile attitude toward groups considered to be their ideological enemies. It is deemed only proper that these latter groups be deprived of access to, and influence over, the holders of governmental power.

---

[12] This section relies heavily upon the study by Joseph La Palombara, *Interest Groups in Italian Politics,* University of Princeton Press, Princeton, N.J., 1964.

Interest groups focus on the legislature much more than in Britain because the bureaucracy is more biased in favor of certain major groups and parties as against others. Furthermore, interest groups are virtually constituent elements of the different political parties in the legislature, and the legislature is more important as an independent policy-making institution than is the Parliament in Britain.

Administration, Party, and Interest Groups: Lobbying in the Bureaucracy

The power of the public administration to fill out and implement the law bestows upon the bureaucracy tremendous power. The bureaucracy has a major voice in rule-making as well as rule application that makes it important for groups to intervene in administrative decision-making. Moreover, since red tape and confusion characterize Italian public administration, groups that can cut through this red tape to expedite, hinder, or modify administrative actions and rulings possess a great advantage.

Ministers and the bureaucracy, the political heads and the civil service apparatus in charge of public administration, afford unequal access to interest groups. An identification with the dominant political party in the government is the single most important source of access for interest groups desiring to exert influence within the administration. Joseph La Palombara refers to this relationship as *parentela*. The Catholic interest groups in labor, agriculture, and other areas of society that associate with the Christian Democratic Party, the long-time dominant party controlling the government, are greatly favored over others in access to, and treatment by, the ministers and the bureaucracy. The bureaucracy is not neutral as in Britain, nor is it shielded from domination by the principal political party. It is highly sensitive to that party and, consequently, grants favorable treatment to those interest groups allied with the party. Interest groups on the margins of this party or those identified with opposing parties must place special emphasis upon representation in the national legislature because they are discriminated against in the administrative sector.

A second pattern of interrelationships between administration and interest groups has been designated as *clientela* by La Palombara. It involves close relations between the bureaucracy of an agency and an interest group recognized by the former as the proper spokesman and representative of that sector of society with which the agency is concerned. Again this leads to unequal access to the ministries, special treatment, favoritism in the consultative committee structure, and partiality in filling jobs. *Clientela* poses its own set of special problems for interest groups, in that few can speak as the authoritative representative for any sector of society; ideology divides them too much. Yet, each desires to profit from a *clientela* relationship.

Because the Italian public administration is inadequately staffed, *clientela* groups are in a position to exert even more influence. Many of the interest groups have extensive research staffs and trained specialists in their organizations. As a result, the bureaucracy is dependent for information and expertise upon interest groups and not vice versa. When groups develop more superior technical facilities than the executive, itself, the rules of the bureaucracy are often expressions of narrowly organized interest groups. When, moreover, the national legislature calls upon the bureaucracy for technical information, much of it comes from the data supplied by the interest groups. Those groups frozen out of *clientela* or *parentela* relationships are, in effect, excluded from the tremendous power wielded by the executives in the political system. They are forced to turn to legislative lobbying as a means for gaining representation in the decision-making process.

Party, Legislature, and Interest Groups

Other elements in the political system make interest group intervention in the legislature desirable. Employment of the "list" system of proportional representation at election time ensures a fairly accurate representation in the legislature of a large number of parties. A most important strategy for interest groups is one that secures them direct representation in Parliament through the political parties. Not only do interest groups seek such representation but they are encouraged by parties to work through their ranks and to send their leaders as party candidates to the legislature.

Groups seek parties that are ideologically similar. For example, left wing unions and women's groups have strong representation in the national executives and legislative ranks of the Communist and socialist parties. Conservative interest groups representing small and medium farmers, the Catholic Action representing the primary mass socio-political instrument of the church, and the Catholic trade union confederation have won strong representation in the Christian Democratic Party organization as well as in its parliamentary party.

Political party is the key determinant of voting in the legislature. Interest groups may organize their own parliamentary blocs or rely upon legislative members of their profession or occupation to articulate and represent their views in the legislative process, but the parties insist upon discipline and unity on policy matters in Parliament. Direct representation of interest groups does not, therefore, necessarily lead to interest group legislators acting on their own, apart from party, on policy questions. However, these legislators do play important roles in bringing the interest groups' views to their party colleagues, leaders, and the party caucuses.

La Palombara suggests that there is no real substitute for direct representation of interest groups in the legislature. The major big-industry association in Italy, Confindustria, which has excellent *clientela* relations in a part of the bureaucracy, finds itself at a distinct disadvantage in the legislature since it has very little direct representation there. Groups associated with the dominant party in the government, of course, are able to maximize their leverage considerably over rule-making. Interest groups that secure representation in the legislature through the opposition parties also find that they possess valuable advantages over those groups that must approach the legislature from outside its membership.

Strategies, Tactics and Opportunities for Affecting the Legislature and Its Decisions

Groups that are represented inside the legislature and those that lobby from outside its membership have recourse to a number of strategies and tactics for influencing legislative actions and decisions.

(A) CONFERENCES A general conference on particular items of importance for public policy is often utilized to provide the program of the group with an aura of public interest. The conference, to which legislators are invited, is an endeavor to overcome the narrow ideological basis of the interest groups, to impress upon legislators that group claims come from a much broader public than the particular interest group, itself.

(B) CAMPAIGN ASSISTANCE Active, even massive support by interest groups in election campaigns—money, propaganda, the solicitation of votes—is not only common among the major groups but is accepted as legitimate. The interest group hopes, of course, that those whom it supports will reciprocate to its advantage in the legislative process.

(C) PROVIDING INFORMATION TO LEGISLATORS The Italian legislature, like the bureaucracy, has almost no research and secretarial resources of its own. Legislators must go outside the legislature for detailed information on programs. By providing such assistance, an interest group can influence the details and, possibly, the frame of reference within which they are employed in legislation. And in return for its assistance, it can expect a sympathetic ear when it comes to the legislature with its own proposals.

(D) LOBBYING WITH INDIVIDUAL MEMBERS   Members may be asked by an interest group to speak, vote, present amendments, and work for its goals with their party colleagues on legislative committees. Because party counts the most in Parliament, those interest groups that can reach the party leaders have a better chance for marshaling strength in the legislature. Influential party members as well as rank and file are also lobbied. Few groups, however, lobby with legislators of different ideological leanings. The Italian Association of Entertainers, which does, is a rare example of a mixed ideological group. Socialists, Communists, Fascists, and Christian Democrats belong to its parliamentary faction. Of course, it does not raise major issues of importance.

In lobbying the legislators, the interest groups are also aware that party discipline is not absolute. Party leaders may insist that their followers comply with the decisions of their party caucuses, but the final vote in Parliament is by secret ballot; deputies have deviated on occasion from the party line. Moreover, the Italian political culture is very permissive regarding lobbying tactics in the legislature. Except for party influences, the self-discipline of ideology, and laws against out-and-out bribery, almost no limitations are imposed upon lobbyists. In contrast with Great Britain, lobbyists in Italy may resort to threats and inducements, economic as well as electoral.

(E) LOBBYING IS FACILITATED BY THE ORGANIZATION AND OPERATION OF PARLIAMENT   Particular features of the legislature make lobbying in the Italian Parliament much more profitable than in the British House of Commons. Unlike the British Parliament, both legislative chambers in Italy have almost equal power; laws have to be passed in identical form. Hence, interest groups have a greater opportunity to affect or curb legislation dealing with major and minor policy issues or with technical matters. Most important, the two legislative chambers are composed of a number of specialized standing committees which have important powers. Intervention in the committee, *per se,* is an integral aspect of the lobbying process. Most legislation is actually adopted at this point, and the legislation which is passed along to Parliament for consideration is also affected by the committee process.

By a majority vote, the legislative committees in the Italian Parliament can enact legislation into law. This procedure is called *sede deliberante*. Certain legislation may not be considered in such a manner: treaties, taxes, the budget, public expenditures, constitutional proposals, elections. Although major bills on public policy are not left to committees, less significant or technical legislation can have important consequences for interest groups. Over two thirds of the government-sponsored bills and 90 per cent of private member bills become law by committee action alone. The *sede deliberante* affords organized interests "considerable leverage over the legislative process."[13]

Interest groups have an additional incentive in maintaining strong connections with legislative committees that handle bills of concern to them. If they can influence the choice of the *relatore* of the committee, they can exercise some control over its procedures and proposals. Since this officer is responsible for assembling the technical information on a legislative proposal, he can select the groups and sources from which to obtain his information. He can delay or expedite the movement of bills to the chamber for debate. And it is he who delivers the major speech on the bill that is reported out of committee. The response in the chamber to the bill may be influenced significantly by this speech and the documentation which he presents.

Interest Groups and the Political System in the United States

Inasmuch as we are abstracting only the critical aspects of political systems relevant to lobbying by interest groups, five features of the system in the United States shall be examined.

An Absence of Ideology

The first is the absence of ideology in the American political culture. Ours is not a society highly fragmented by ideological divisions; it is more comparable to that of Britain rather than Italy. The basics in our political and economic system are taken for granted and accepted as legitimate by the major contending forces in the society.

One type of documentation of this consensus is provided by Gabriel A. Almond and Sidney Verba in their comparative study of civic cultures.[14] Surveying political attitudes in five nations, the authors factored out a series of responses regarding partisanship that are relevant to our inquiry. Adherents of parties who are extremely hostile to each other were said to reflect a culture which is highly divided. Partisanship is limited when individuals can accept the

[13] *Ibid.*, p. 110.
[14] Gabriel A. Almond and Sidney Verba, *The Civic Culture; Political Attitudes and Democracy in Five Nations,* Princeton University Press, Princeton, N.J., 1963.

adherents of other political parties and regard them as respectable persons similar to themselves. In such cultures, there is more that unites individuals than separates them. When Republican and Democratic supporters were asked, for example, to attribute positive and negative qualities to voters of these parties, a large proportion ascribed the same qualities of patriotism, intelligence, and humanitarianism to members of the opposite party as well as their own. In Great Britain, a somewhat sharper polarization was evident, whereas Italian party members were extremely critical of members of other parties.

When supporters of the major parties were queried regarding their reaction to the possible marriage of their children across party lines, the overwhelming majority of Republicans and Democrats expressed indifference. The Conservatives in Britain were somewhat more concerned, but Italian Christian Democrats reacted very strongly against interparty marriage. Almond and Verba concluded that attitudes of interpersonal trust and cooperation are much more frequent in the United States and Britain and that these general social attitudes penetrate the realm of politics. They inhibit political fragmentation and represent an important consensual norm that one's private group ought not to be politicized. They foster a "form of partisanship that is tolerant of opposition, ambiguity and contingency."[15]

Apropos of ideology, itself, careful studies on the American voter suggest that political attitudes toward domestic issues are better understood if notions of ideology are discarded in favor of "primitive self-interest."[16] "Ideologues" represent merely a deviant few among the members of the Democratic and Republican parties. The "types of attitude structure presumed in ideological accounts of political behavior are not very prevalent in the American electorate."[17]

Neither the American legislator nor the American voter is committed to, or acts primarily upon, ideological grounds. "The barrenness of ideology in political socialization . . . ." William J. Keefe and Morris S. Ogul have pointed out, "is suggestive regarding legislators' relations with political interest groups."[18] If ideology is of such little significance, or the legislators are tied so loosely to it, they may more

[15] *Ibid.*, p. 134.

[16] Angus Campbell, Philip E. Converse, Warren E. Miller, and Donald E. Stokes, *The American Voter,* John Wiley & Sons, Inc., New York, 1960, pp. 203–09.

[17] *Ibid.*, p. 215.

[18] William J. Keefe and Morris S. Ogul, *The American Legislative Process: Congress and the States,* Prentice-Hall, Englewood, N.J., 1964, p. 307.

easily respond to the demands of interest groups. Because, with rare exceptions, the American groups themselves are not ideological, bargaining with them can be conducted on a pragmatic basis. Under such circumstances and, in the absence of highly disciplined parties, students of the American legislative process have contended that: "It is plausible to suppose that pressure groups are the principal beneficiaries of the low ideological content in the typical legislator's outlook."[19]

American politics is highly pragmatic and strongly personality oriented. American parties tend to aggregate interests and articulate claims; they try to adjust them within their own ranks before they approach the decision centers of the legislature and the executive. At the same time, interest groups feel free to push forward on their own in the legislature and in the executive without being tied to, or isolated from, either major party. Certain groups do tend to be more closely associated with each of the parties—for example, the AMA and the U.S. Chamber of Commerce with the Republican Party and the AFL-CIO, Farmers' Union, and Negro groups with the Democratic Party. But there is nothing comparable to the ideological ties between interest groups and parties which exist in Italy. Groups forge temporary alliances with other interest groups in the absence of ideological inhibitors, and groups cooperate with members and leaders of both the major parties.

Interest groups that are nonideological can join with a party on one issue and oppose it on another. The AMA, for example, consistently worked to frustrate the Kennedy and Johnson administrations' efforts to secure the adoption of medical insurance legislation for the aged during the period, 1961–65. At the same time, it participated with the Democratic Administration and legislative leaders in joint efforts on behalf of federal aid for medical education. The U.S. Chamber of Commerce and the American Farm Bureau Federation have frequently opposed Democratic-sponsored legislation. Yet both worked with the Kennedy Administration in its congressional campaign for passage of the 1962 Trade Expansion Act to which the Administration had assigned the highest priority.

Democracy and Localism

The political culture in the United States accords great respect to both democracy and localism. The predominant conception of representation emphasizes local constituencies and the importance of public

[19] *Idem.*

opinion. A legislator is expected to concern himself with representing the people in his constituency, guarding their interests, and securing for them a variety of benefits. In part, this attitude constitutes a unique development that emphasis upon mass democracy has produced in the United States: The people in their separate localities are to be directly represented by legislators who speak primarily for them, not for party or class. It also stems from constitutional mandates and certain operational aspects of politics. In each state the electorate can vote for a chief executive and/or a set of executives, who represent state constituencies, and a double set of legislators (except for Nebraska), who represent the interests and concerns of different constituencies. An identical pattern pertains to elected national officials, except for the fact that only the President and Vice President are elected as executives. At the same time, the political "rules of the game" dictate that representatives be selected from within local units and elected by them, and generally on the basis of local constituency considerations.

A deep concern for public opinion, or at least the opinions of publics in the local constituencies, is one of the characteristics of the political system. Spokesmen for private groups who seek to influence legislation and administration, V. O. Key, Jr., has stated, operate "in a milieu of concern about opinion either actual or latent."[20] This concern predisposes legislators as well as executives to attend to all shades of opinions and preferences and to listen to lobbyists. Because interest groups endeavor to make certain that the opinions of their publics are articulated, such groups fit legitimately into the framework of concern for public opinion within which public decision-makers operate.

Fragmentation of Government: Federalism

The political system is also characterized by an extreme diffusion of power among the official decision-makers. This fragmentation exposes all the facets and levels of government to interest group activity and also focuses much of such activity on the legislative process.

Federalism has imposed one major set of divisions in the system. Important powers of government belong constitutionally and, therefore, independently to the fifty states. The national government is invested with tremendous powers of its own. And both levels of government are bound intimately together in a vast system of cooperative programs involving national finances and standards as well as

[20] V. O. Key, Jr., *Public Opinion and American Democracy*, Alfred A. Knopf, Inc., New York, 1961, p. 530.

state administration and financing. Cities, too, are tied to the national government in comparable sets of relationships, some of which bypass the state governments. Interest groups concerned with the operation of such programs or seeking the establishment of new programs must operate at both major levels of the federal system and, sometimes, at the local level of the county and city.

One result of this system is that cities and states increasingly assume roles of institutional interest groups. Cities, at the state level, and cities as well as states, at the national level, have a great deal at stake in decisions regarding existing programs or new ones. Not only is a powerful League of Municipalities active in each state but the U.S. Conference of Mayors and the American Municipal Association speak with some force in the national executive and legislature. These associations have established their own lobbying organizations for this purpose. A new type of permanent lobby in Washington, D.C., is that established independently of such associations by more and more of the major cities and states which have concluded that the protection of their interests requires them to conduct their own lobbying through their own staffs.

A second consequence is that interest groups have a greater variety of strategies available to them. They may operate at either the state or national level or at both simultaneously; indeed, some may be compelled to because they seek, or are affected, by programs at both levels. Should they fail at one level, they may focus on the other. For example, many educational interest groups have discovered that they must lobby actively in the national government. The central government has increasingly become a partner in public school and university education through its financial support although education has traditionally been a state-local function.

To the extent that states are independent governments with important powers, interest groups can achieve substantial results at this level. Such accomplishments are also important for group morale, unity, and leadership. At the same time, group leaders are afforded an opportunity to master the techniques of lobbying should they be compelled to intervene in the national government with its more complicated system. The Anti-Saloon League achieved many of its objectives initially in the states before its final campaign for prohibition at the national level. Its state experience served it well as an apprenticeship for national politics, for, in the process, it learned what was effective and what was not. In contrast, the OARP, Ltd., the initial Townsend corporation, was thrust prematurely into national politics by the nature of its demands. Its leaders had neither built up a significant political base nor acquired sufficient experience in lobbying. Their extremely inept performance in the Congress was attributable, in part, to this inadequacy.

An additional aspect of the relationship between federalism and interest groups arises from the fact that specific groups exercise more influence at one level of government than another. The "states' rights" argument has often been advanced as a cloak by those groups which have considered themselves disadvantaged in the national decision-making centers and at an advantage in the states.[21] Of course, in a universe of fifty states, a group may be disadvantaged in one state and at the national level but wield considerable influence in other states. For years until 1964, groups which pushed for the adoption of FEPC legislation were thwarted in the Congress. No state legislature or governor in the South would even consider such a proposal. But in a number of northern cities and states, these groups were strong enough, either by themselves or in cooperation with a political party, to secure the adoption of antidiscrimination legislation pertaining to housing, employment, and public facilities.

The attention of city governments and many urban-based groups has, to a significant extent, been directed toward the national government as a matter of political necessity. State legislatures have been notoriously gerrymandered—covertly or overtly—in favor of rural elements, a situation which conservative and business interest groups have found particularly suitable to their own ends. On the other hand, urban, ethnic, minority, and labor groups have been extremely disadvantaged in many state legislatures. In fact, one reason for the battle to overturn the Supreme Court's decision applying the one-man-one-vote principle to both houses of state legislatures stems from the bitter opposition of groups that have a vested interest in retaining rural, conservative-dominated state legislatures. They recognize that the court's ruling will divert power and influence from them to others.

Fragmentation of Government: The Separation of Powers and Checks and Balances

The American political system separates the executive from the legislature, making each responsible to different electorates and assigning to each distinct responsibilities. At the same time, it involves each in the powers or functions of the other. Except for Nebraska,

21 Robert J. Harris, "States' Rights and Vested Interests," *Journal of Politics,* Vol. 15, No. 4, November 1953, p. 467.

American legislatures, state and national, are also divided into two chambers of roughly equal power. Thus, within the federal system, government is fragmented further, with the different power centers that are responsible for making authoritative decisions confronting each other. Built-in conflict is engendered by different outlooks, responsibilities, constituencies, and "mandates in time." While interest groups are afforded an expanded range of opportunities to intervene profitably, they face an impressive series of obstacles if they attempt to move all these branches of government in unison.

The executive is much more complex and confusing in the American system than in that of Italy or Great Britain. The governors and the President are the chief executives of their governments. Nevertheless, on the state level, at least, a number of executives are often independently elected by the voters. In some states, voters may choose not only a governor but also a number of the following: an attorney general, a commissioner of agriculture, a superintendent of public instruction, a commissioner of insurance, a secretary of state, a comptroller, and a variety of other officials. Each has his own position, tenure, and functions, with little responsibility to the others. Different executives may represent different political parties or different factions within the same party.

Strategy directed at the executive is mandatory for interest groups that want to secure new policies, alter existing laws in substantive ways, or prevent change. The chief executive has evolved into the most important initiating force in public policy. Without his support, or in the face of his opposition, an interest group that wants to obtain major legislation is at a decided disadvantage.

The legislature can not only alter or refuse to adopt legislation proposed by the executive but it is, itself, an independent center for originating legislation. Each legislator may introduce whatever and as many bills, of a private or public nature, that he wishes. Few interest groups, therefore, can afford to ignore the legislature with its extensive power over finances, its ability to write or rewrite the rules of public policy, or to determine administrative organization and procedures.

Groups seeking to impede the adoption of new public policies must include the legislature in their strategy as an independent locus of power. At the national level and in many of the states, it is not only equivalent to the executive in the constitutional power it exerts regarding legislation but also it is organizationally better suited for negating, rather than instituting, new policy proposals. Groups sponsoring new policies or alterations in existing laws must also concentrate on these institutions of government since a variety of legislative hurdles must be overcome before legislation is adopted.

The importance of committees in the Congress and in most state legislatures cannot be overemphasized. In comparison with the few nonspecialized committees in Britain, which may merely refine bills already debated and approved in the cabinet and in the House of Commons, and committees of the Italian legislature, which are not permitted to act conclusively on major legislation, the American committee is virtually *sui generis*. In the Congress and in many state legislatures, committees can refuse to accommodate themselves to the program of the executives; they can ignore the wishes of the dominant party in the legislature; they can change, consider, or initiate legislation on their own. As the specialized subsystems of the legislature, they are respected as well as authoritative loci of power.

With rare exceptions, therefore, interest groups must concern themselves with committees if they wish to influence public policy. Committees headed by sympathetic chairmen and majorities simplify their tasks; an antagonistic chairman or committee is a real road block.

Committees constitute only one stage in the legislative process. At subsequent points, opportunities are available for altering or defeating legislation; and, in the American two-house legislatures, approximately the same procedure must be duplicated in each house. Because the legislative process, itself, furnishes maximum opportunities and advantages for groups that would delay, alter, or defeat legislation, an intensive effort is required from groups sponsoring controversial legislation. Such legislation must often proceed to the final conference committee, back to the legislature, on to the chief executive, and return to the legislature for extraordinary majorities if a veto is to be overridden.

Interest groups must concern themselves with the legislature for still another reason: its power to intervene and exercise control over the bureaucracy. Unlike the parliaments of Great Britain and Italy, American legislatures insist upon the right to probe deeply or widely, at any time, into the administrative sector of government and to investigate for partisan reasons as well as to assert the legislative claim of supremacy over the administration of policy. American legislatures indulge in the practice of legislating in detail on rules, procedures, policy, and the organization of the bureaucracy. Furthermore, administrative decisions are often overridden via the legislative appropriations process.

The administrative side of the executive is also vital to interest groups, as we note in a subsequent chapter. However, the bureaucracy does not enjoy that favorable position which characterizes public administration in Britain and on the continent. American legislatures are inclined to be suspicious of the bureaucracy and intervene in its affairs to control, regulate, and interfere with its operations. The majority political party does not provide that political protection afforded the bureaucracy in Britain or even in Italy. Hence, the legislature is a focal point for appealing bureaucratic decisions, for intimidating the bureaucracy, and for obtaining support for that part of the bureaucracy which interest groups favor. In turn, the administrative agencies of government must cultivate the power centers in the legislature for their own survival and growth.

An Absence of Disciplined Parties

When we note also an absence of disciplined political parties, the relevant general characteristics of the American system for politically interested groups stands out in even sharper relief against those of Britain and Italy. State legislatures are not renowned for their partisan spirit or cohesion. A 1954 study disclosed the existence of strong party spirit and cohesion in the legislatures of seventeen states, occasional or moderate party cohesion in those of eleven states, and weak or no party cohesion in twenty states.[22] The same pattern appears to prevail today. In a 1963 study of four state legislative systems, the authors found that partisanship and the impact of party on the legislative process was greatest in New Jersey, less so in Ohio, and much less so in California and Tennessee.[23]

The U.S. Congress also reflects this general American phenomenon. From a series of round-table discussions with members of the House of Representatives, Charles L. Clapp concluded that their parties "fall far short of being well-disciplined powerful organizations, possessing the means for effective permanent enforcement of sanctions against recalcitrant members. . . ."[24] Party leadership is extremely diffused and often contradictory. At least three sets of leaders exist: Those chosen by their party; those automatically elevated to com-

[22] Belle Zeller, ed., *American State Legislatures,* Thomas Y. Crowell Co., New York, 1954, pp. 192 *ff.*

[23] John C. Wahlke, Heinz Eulau, William Buchanan, and LeRoy C. Ferguson, *The Legislative System, Explorations in Legislative Behavior,* John Wiley & Sons, Inc., New York, 1962, Chapter 15, "The Legislator and His Party: Majority and Minority."

[24] Charles L. Clapp, *The Congressman, His Work As He Sees It,* The Brookings Institution, Washington, D.C., 1963, p. 313.

mittee chairmanship by the seniority system; and those listened to because of personal influence and expertise on particular issues.

The leadership is not united, and frequently individual committee chairmen cooperate with minority party members against the majority party leaders. The combination of individuals involved in the "leadership" may change from issue to issue. Moreover, party leadership, as represented by the Speaker and the majority leaders and whips in the House and Senate, is more personal than institutional. This has meant that party leaders, especially, and committee leaders, to a lesser extent, must rely on personality, favors, compromises, and adjustments; their ability to act as brokers among members and between blocs is vital to their effective functioning as leaders.

Party leaders can invoke certain sanctions against members, a fact which is recognized by individual legislators and which maximizes the influence of the leadership. But discipline is rarely invoked when a member finds himself unable or unwilling to "go along" on particular issues.[25] The most drastic type of sanction that party leaders have employed against legislative members of their party, loss of seniority, has been imposed on legislators for supporting the presidential candidate of the opposing party during the general election—not because the dissident legislators voted in opposition to the party leaders in the legislature.

The leadership needs and seeks the support of those interest groups normally identified with their party. Without such aid, they can sometimes be defeated in their own chambers. Congressmen attribute the defeat of a gas bill, in which Democratic Speaker Sam Rayburn was vitally interested and for which he thought he had the votes, to widespread defection among supposedly committed members who were susceptible to labor's influence.[26] Labor intervened a day before the bill came to a vote and dissolved the majority which the leadership in the House had carefully constructed.

Despite the fact that the party leadership is neither unified nor institutionally powerful, most congressmen tend to support their party's positions. On the basis of his study of the Eighty-first Congress, David B. Truman concluded that party label is the "single most reliable indicator of congressional voting behavior."[27] Congressmen are disposed to support their party's position because of their philosophical outlook, their commitments, and their respect for the

---

[25] *Ibid.,* p. 288.

[26] *Ibid.,* pp. 287–88.

[27] David B. Truman, *The Congressional Party, A Case Study,* John Wiley & Sons, Inc., New York, 1959, p. 247.

leadership and its affect on the course of legislation.[28] A chief executive's appeal to party spirit also tends to introduce new cohesive elements into the ranks of his party in the legislature.

Legislators act independently of their parties when they assess the parties' position on issues as undercutting their chances for reelection, when they view such a suggested course as harmful to the interests of their constituencies, or when their beliefs conflict sharply with the party position staked out by the leadership. Legislative leaders generally recognize these grounds as being legitimate when a legislator refuses to conform to their policies.

Legislators, in the Congress and in the great majority of states, are dependent upon local party units for nomination and election and often upon nonparty sources for campaign financing. In some states, the primary throws the party wide open to intervention by a variety of groups in the election districts. In others, local party leaders exercise much greater control over the selection machinery.[29] But in both cases, the political processes produce candidates who must meet the basic qualifications of the districts in which they live.

The national image of his party may injure a legislator. The disastrous impact upon the careers of Republican congressional and state legislative candidates by the 1964 campaign of their presidential nominee, Barry Goldwater, illustrates V. O. Key's observation that the individual legislator benefits or suffers from the general approval or disapproval of the performance of his party. He may be held accountable not as an individual but as a member of a larger entity, his party.[30] Nevertheless, the recurrent problem of winning reelection makes the legislator very conscious of his source of office—his constituency. Clapp found that congressmen as a whole accorded "constituency work," in behalf of individuals and groups in the local electorate, precedence over their legislative work. Similarly, the comparative study of four state legislative systems found legislators deeply involved with pursuing service functions for their constituents.

James M. Burns has characterized one extreme representative type as a "Pressure Politician," the legislator so acutely sensitive to the predominant interests of his constituency that he acts "instinctively" as a representative of the groups that articulate these interests and often before such groups initiate action.[31] The more homogeneous

---

[28] Clapp, *op. cit.*, p. 313.

[29] Frank J. Sorauf, *Party and Representation, Legislative Politics in Pennsylvania*, Atherton Press, New York, 1963.

[30] V. O. Key, *op. cit.*, p. 498. See also Truman, *op. cit.*, pp. 194–95.

[31] James M. Burns, *Congress on Trial, The Politics of Modern Law Making*, Harper & Brothers, New York, 1949, Chapter II, "The Pressure Politicians."

a constituency, the more likely that on one or two issues, at least, its representative may be circumscribed in his freedom of action within the legislature should he not, in fact, already adhere to these views himself.

Our main point here is that he is relatively free from national or state party discipline and more dependent upon local finances and upon the local party, which is generally less interested in issues than it is in winning elections. He is relatively free, therefore, to vote for what he believes to be important to his reelection and to the interests of his district or to vote in accordance with his own convictions. Apropos of national legislators, the national party has no control over their running for office or their nomination; only indirectly does it influence their chances for reelection. In terms of our study of comparative political systems, the American legislator is a "free" agent. This makes him much more amenable and accessible to the appeals, ideas, and offers·of interest groups.

Interest groups can and do contribute significantly in election campaigns. Their endorsement can provide a candidate with the proper exposure in his constituency; often their endorsement makes him acceptable to members of other groups. Their work in his behalf can furnish him with the necessary campaign machinery and assist in the turnout of additional favorable votes. Campaigns are expensive undertakings in the United States, the cost of which increases with the size of the constituency. By providing financial assistance, interest groups can help candidates cover these onerous expenses and also circumvent the unrealistically restrictive monetary limits imposed by laws dealing with electioneering.

Only a few interest groups engage in national or state-wide campaign politics to select or elect candidates. Commencing with the formation of the CIO's Political Action Committee, in 1943, organized labor turned to grass roots campaigning as a means for ensuring the election of sympathetic legislators and executives at the local, state, and national levels. Today, the AFL-CIO operates in campaign politics through its Committee on Political Education (COPE).[32]

What does COPE offer candidates that they seek its endorsement? COPE invests a large part of its finances and energies in increasing the number of registered voters and in bringing them to the polls. It has offered candidates not merely financial contributions but mass organizational support—a vital asset to any campaign, and one which neither business groups nor the local political party can effectively muster in many communities. Where its members are

[32] Mary G. Zon, "Labor in Politics," *Law and Contemporary Problems,* Vol. XXVII, No. 2, Spring, 1962, pp. 234–51.

concentrated in constituencies, COPE mobilizes them in intensive door-to-door campaigning. By contributing money to candidates outside its areas of membership concentration, it assists sympathetic legislators seeking reelection who do not consider labor's endorsement the "kiss of death." In addition, it has engaged in educational and propaganda campaigns as have individual unions.

COPE claims to have helped elect 73.7 per cent of those candidates for Congress and gubernatorial offices, in 1960, whom it judged to have a reasonable chance to win and thus were furnished maximum assistance.[33] In one of its most successful campaigns, the renomination of Senator Estes Kefauver, in 1960, COPE members made 60,000 telephone calls, mailed 300,000 pieces of literature, distributed 160,000 leaflets, and established a central file of 65,000 union members in Tennessee.[34] In southern states where labor has been traditionally weak in the legislatures, COPE has tied a carefully designed package of legislative goals to its political potential in what is called "Programs of Progress"; and it has achieved some success in Louisiana, Tennessee, and Arkansas. In 1961, for example, COPE endorsements were sought for the first time by candidates for the Mississippi state legislature.

Obviously a substantial fraction of union members differ with their leaders when the latter seek their votes for endorsed candidates.[35] Although labor leaders cannot guarantee the votes of all their members, they can sometimes provide the extra margin which a candidate needs for his majority. Often labor is tied so closely to the local Democratic Party that the party can afford to ignore its claims upon the candidate selection process. A 1959 study of politics in Philadelphia indicated that, although labor unions made large financial contributions to Democratic candidates, only occasionally had the party permitted itself to be swayed by labor.[36] Because the party's leaders regarded the labor vote as "in the bag" anyway, they ignored or overrode labor's demands for a substantial voice in the selection of candidates. In the Detroit area, on the other hand, labor unions significantly affect policy and the candidate selection processes in the Democratic Party.

[33] *Ibid.*, p. 242.

[34] Nicholas A. Masters, "The Organized Labor Bureaucracy as a Base of Support for the Democratic Party," *Law and Contemporary Problems,* Vol. XXVII, No. 2, Spring, 1962, p. 259; also Zon, *op. cit.*, p. 239.

[35] Samuel Lubell, *The Future of American Politics,* Harper & Brothers, New York, 1952, pp. 189–95, for what happened when the union leadership tried to eliminate Senator Robert A. Taft of Ohio in 1950.

[36] James Reichley, *The Art of Government, Reform, and Organization Politics in Philadelphia,* The Fund for the Republic, New York, 1959, pp. 64–66.

Business group leaders have not encountered the problem of raising campaign funds that unions face; therefore, more money is usually available for business-supported candidates. Nonetheless, business groups have achieved little success in competing with unions in organizing independent political organizations of their own and in inducing businessmen to participate actively in local party organizations.[37]

The U.S. Chamber of Commerce has developed a practical politics course through which business leaders are supposed to learn how to become influential in local parties and eventually gain a voice in candidate selection. Numerous corporations and local chambers have supported such courses. However, an assessment of one major effort by the Manufacturers' Association of Syracuse (N.Y.) to activate middle-level corporate leaders to participate in political parties concluded that the results were disappointingly small in proportion to the resources which the sponsoring corporations had invested in this drive. Despite the urging of their superiors, middle-level business leaders were reluctant to take part in local politics. And local politicians remained skeptical of the entire experiment.

At times, business interest groups have set up special political organizations to campaign for specific issues or candidates. In 1961, the U.S. Chamber of Commerce created a Special Committee for Voluntary Unionism to work for the passage of "right-to-work" laws. The AMA, whose policy positions generally coincide with those of the business community, created its own Political Action Committee in July 1961; some state medical societies also organized such committees to support candidates. In its 1949–50 efforts to frustrate the enactment of national health insurance legislation, the AMA and its public relations firm encouraged local doctors to set up campaign committees that participated directly in a number of elections.[38] "Doctors for Dulles" worked closely with Republican state leaders in New York and involved over 10,000 doctors in that state in an unsuccessful campaign to elect John Foster Dulles, the Republican candidate, to the United States Senate.

Interest groups that endorse and campaign for candidates cannot always be certain of the support these candidates will provide them once they have been elected. Sometimes this reflects the varying degrees of commitment which group leaders accept in return for their endorsements. But even sympathetic legislators do not always prove

[37] Andrew Hacker and Joel D. Aberbach, "Businessmen in Politics," *Law and Contemporary Problems,* Vol. XXVII, No. 2, Spring, 1962, pp. 266–79.
[38] Stanley Kelley, Jr., *Professional Public Relations and Political Power,* The Johns Hopkins Press, Baltimore, 1956, pp. 87–89.

as cooperative as the group wishes them to be. The relations between the Townsendites and their endorsed congressmen at critical junctures in the legislative process illustrate this problem.

In the period 1936–44, a large number of candidates for Congress sought Townsend endorsements, and the pension leaders and their clubs worked actively for many of them. After the 1938 election, Townsendites claimed to have elected 134 endorsed candidates to the House of Representatives. On a roll-call vote on the Townsend bill, in 1939, only 54 per cent of the Townsend bloc (seventy-three) voted for the bill; fifty-nine, or 44 per cent, opposed it. In 1944, the Townsendites needed only one additional name on a discharge petition in order to extract their bill from committee; so confident were the Townsend leaders that they met to plan their floor strategy. However, four legislators withdrew their names, and the session terminated with only 213 signatures, five short. Thirteen endorsed legislators had failed to sign the petition. In the Eightieth Congress, Republican Congressman Harold Knutson (Minn.), who had voted for the Townsend bills of 1935 and 1939 and had been continuously reendorsed, became chairman of the Committee on Ways and Means. Nevertheless, he refused to use the powers of his office to assist the Townsend bill in any way.

In the final analysis, the political underpinnings of this group's endorsement policy were weak. Its leaders had accepted almost any sort of commitment in their attempt to elect a sympathetic group of legislators. However, regardless of which group intervenes in the election process, when it endorses a large number of candidates, it can never be confident that its partisan involvement in election campaigns will produce the results it desires in the legislative process.

The Example of California: Weak Parties Plus Non-Partisan Executives Equal Strong Interest Groups

The tremendous influence that interest groups can bring to bear upon public policy in a legislative environment devoid of effective executive leadership and virtually any party identification is exemplified by the experience of California, especially in the period 1943–51.[39] Although California represented a deviant case among legislatures, it demonstrated the advantages that accrue to interest groups if certain elements in the political culture are carried to their extremes.

During this period, the major parties were notoriously weak and loosely organized in the California legislature. The legislature repre-

---

[39] William Buchanan, *Legislative Partisanship, The Deviant Case of California,* University of California Press, Berkeley, 1963.

sented a situation of nonpartisanship rather than partisanship although the governor and a majority of both houses were Republicans. Over one half of the candidates for the legislature were "elected" in primaries as a result of cross-filing, a system wherein a candidate could compete simultaneously for nomination by a number of parties. The nominating system encouraged candidates to file in the primaries of both major parties, since nomination in both meant *de facto* election. Such being the case, a candidate's chances for election were enhanced by his ability to blur his party image; a strong party image was an obvious disadvantage in a great many legislative districts. Most candidates for state-wide executive offices also sought the nomination of more than one party. Political parties suffered, moreover, from a general unfavorable image in the California political culture. In 1949, they were, in general, poorly organized and impotent.

Not only did candidates seeking nominations have to raise their own campaign funds but once they were nominated, the state party paid them little consideration; its interests centered on the top of the ticket. Virtually no money was available to legislative candidates for the expenses of campaigning other than their personal funds and such as nonparty groups and friends would provide. "The cost of the election," concluded a student of this period, "was perhaps the widest chink in the armor of the legislator."[40] And it was one about which the well-financed lobbyists in Sacramento were well aware.

Contributions of hundreds of dollars from interest groups to legislators were customary in this period. The chain store lobby alone, in 1936, was reported to have written checks ranging from $100 to $500 which thirty assembly candidates accepted. It invested a total of $10,000 in candidate contributions and, significantly, both the majority and minority leaders in the legislature accepted such aid.

In the legislature, candidates for the speakership of the assembly, always of the majority party, bargained with members of the minority party for the necessary votes to win a majority. Their own parties were too factionalized to make the choice themselves. Without party lines to divide the vote, the outcome was never comfortably predictable. Interest groups that had helped legislators win election often made few demanding claims upon them except for their votes on the speakership. By helping to trade votes for a speaker, interest groups were rewarded by being granted a voice in deciding who chaired and composed the legislative committees. There were few restrictions imposed upon the speaker by his party and few party

[40] *Ibid.,* p. 22.

guide lines by which his actions could be assessed. In addition, votes by minority members could be rewarded, for the speaker frequently gave chairmanships and, occasionally, even a majority membership on certain committees to minority party members. One legislator is reported as having described how the speaker ought to act on appointments in the following terms: "He should be fair to party, to area, to the membership, and to the Third House [the lobbies]."[41] Quite a few speakers were more than fair to this "Third House."

Interest groups served as brokers between individual legislators and the leadership in helping to choose the latter; between the leadership and legislators in the assignment of chairmen and membership on the standing committees; among speaker, chairmen, committees, and individual members when group claims were pressed. Furthermore, interest groups could marshal votes for individual legislators and their projects. As long as the interest groups and not the parties were judged important by the candidates for their nomination and election, the interest groups could always wield great influence. To this system of influence, which interest groups built up within the nomination, election and legislative spheres, must be added the tremendous amounts spent by these groups for the expenses and entertainment of the legislators in the state's capital.

Artie Samish, the flamboyant kingpin of the California lobbyists in this period, is credited with building a coalition in the legislature that had all the characteristics of a political machine. "He did this by providing some legislators with the twin necessities of their political existence—campaign funds and living expenses."[42] His ability to maneuver in the legislature was enhanced by the fact that the liquor, race track, and business interests that he represented were basically disinterested in general legislation and regulations. They were concerned only with specific taxes and regulations that applied to them. He and the oil interests, which were also very powerful, made minimal demands upon legislators. Except for the speakership and those few issues relevant to the particular groups represented by these lobbyists, the legislators were free to vote as they wished 99 per cent of the time.

Not all the interest groups obtained what they wanted in California. Not all were powerful or fortunate enough to be represented by a master politician such as Samish. But most major interest groups had great influence in negotiating compromises on matters of budget, taxation, and highway policies as well as specific legislation and regulations relating to their own activities.

[41] *Ibid.,* p. 88.
[42] *Ibid.,* p. 43.

CHAPTER 4

Legislators, Lobbyists, and Lobbying

INTEREST GROUPS are one set of external inputs in the legislative process. To achieve any impact therein they must employ pressures or services that legislators find necessary, desirable, or unavoidable. Their lobbyists must exploit opportunities for maneuver afforded by the legislative system in order to overcome obstacles raised against interest group intervention by party, executive leadership, and unfriendly legislative power centers.

The more successfully interest groups accommodate themselves to legislators and the legislative process, in terms of the self-interests and conceptions of the former and the dynamics of the latter, the more rewarding will be their activities, the more accepted and appreciated their involvement. It is from this conceptual approach that we initiate our discussion of legislative lobbying: Intervention by interest groups in the legislative process. Hence, the principal actors—the legislators—in this decision-making process become our initial focus of attention.

Role Orientations of Legislators Toward Interest Groups and Lobbying

In view of the federal system within which interest groups operate, it is necessary to ascertain the attitude of state as well as national legislators toward lobbying by interest groups. Although most of the fifty state legislatures have not been as systematically studied as has the Congress, a substantial body of research has been built up. The environment of the interest group may vary from legislature to legislature, but it is possible to draw relatively firm generalizations regarding the relationship between legislators and interest groups.

How State Legislators View Lobbying

The only large scale comparative study of legislators and their attitudes toward interest groups is based upon data from four states: California, New Jersey, Ohio, and Tennessee.[1] From the responses

[1] John C. Wahlke, Heinz Eulau, William Buchanan, and LeRoy C. Ferguson, *The Legislative System, Explorations in Legislative Behavior,* John Wiley & Sons, Inc., New York, 1962.

of these lawmakers to queries about interest groups, it is clear that all four legislatures accepted the legitimacy of "pressure politics" by interest groups. On a scale from 0 to 5, the legitimacy of such politics ranged from medium to high: 3.5—Tennessee; 3.8—New Jersey; 4.1—Ohio; 4.4—California.

State legislators adopted different role orientations toward interest groups. On the basis of two indices, attitudes toward, and knowledge of, "pressure groups" (a term used interchangeably with interest groups by the investigators), members in all four legislatures divided into three types: Facilitators, Resisters, and Neutrals. Facilitators were friendly toward interest group activity and evidenced considerable knowledge about it. Resisters were hostile, but, at the same time, relatively knowledgeable. Neutrals either evidenced no strong feelings about interest group activity or, irrespective of their attitudes, possessed little knowledge thereof.

The percentage of Facilitators varied from a low of 23 per cent in Tennessee to a high of 43 per cent in Ohio; California had 38 per cent and New Jersey, 40 per cent. In three states, the percentage of Resisters varied from a low of 20 per cent (California) to a high of 27 per cent (New Jersey); only Tennessee showed a higher proportion, 40 per cent. Out of 305 legislators who could be classified, 124 were Facilitators, 105 Neutrals, and only seventy-six Resisters. Since Neutrals included sympathetic as well as hostile legislators and some Resisters favored one or more interest groups but were hostile in general to all others, attitudes of members of these four legislatures were even more favorable than indicated by the distribution of role types.

All role orientation types overwhelmingly recognized the usefulness of interest groups for the functioning of the legislature: 60 per cent of the Resisters; 80 per cent of the Neutrals; 89 per cent of the Facilitators. Some were even more positive, contending that such groups were *indispensable* to the legislative system. Although only 14 per cent of the Resisters went this far, 39 per cent of the Neutrals as well as 63 per cent of the Facilitators expressed such opinions.

An analysis of Facilitators adds another dimension to our understanding of the receptive legislative environment in which interest groups operate. Facilitators tended to be much more experienced and competent legislators than the other role types. The authors of this study found support for their hypothesis that it was the Facilitators, comprising between 38–43 per cent of the three non-southern legislatures, who acted as the principal vehicles for "pressure" (interest group) politics in the legislative system. Facilitators were more prone to seek out and recognize cues from interest groups and their lobbyists in the legislative process. They were also more ready to use lobbyists in drafting legislation and in marshaling support for their bills.

It is interesting to note that the legislators most sympathetic and sensitive to the desires of the interest groups were the ones least identified with any specific interest group. John C. Wahlke and his associates suggest, therefore, that such legislators acted as arbitrators or umpires because they were not themselves partisans in particular group struggles.

Although a variety of explanations were advanced by members of these state legislatures to justify their listening to the pleas of interest groups, two main classes of reasons predominated. One was the groups' "representational claims," the fact that they represented significant portions of the public. The other was their functional utility, *i.e.,* their "usefulness to the legislature in its lawmaking functions. . . ."[2]

Legislators wanted interest groups to provide them with technical information about bills and problems as well as political information relevant to the implication of bills and their effects upon groups. The members required both types of information, information which they could not otherwise obtain without a great deal of effort. The following types of comments by the legislators revealed this sense of inadequacy on their part: A legislator can't adequately watch all the thousands of bills; he hasn't the staff to assess adequately even the major ones; he does not know the effects of the bills; he does not know everyone's needs. Thus, by providing legislators with services that enable them to operate more successfully, the interest groups gain valuable advantages.

Politically, interest groups enhance their value to legislators by helping them work out compromises and adjustments among the multiplicity of demands from various groups. In view of the conclusion arrived at by Wahlke and associates that the accommodation of interest group demands is a central function of state legislatures, the activities of lobbyists are decidedly functional to the legislative system.

Congressmen and Interest Groups

Similar observations characterize the attitudes of national legislators toward interest groups and their lobbyists. Raymond A. Bauer, Ithiel de Sola Pool, and Lewis A. Dexter, who studied the politics of reciprocal trade legislation of 1953–55, note that vigorous pushing of an interest was regarded by congressmen as perfectly legitimate.[3] Not only did most congressmen believe strongly in the right of petition but they regarded many of the communications which came to their offices as helpful and instructive. Legislators stood in great need of information and assistance, either because they were partisans of an issue or because they encountered difficulties in making up their minds. In other words, communications from interest groups were considered functional to the legislators' ability to operate effectively in the congressional system.

More often than not, congressmen indicated that they welcomed communications from lobbyists. Some actually sought out lobbyists to obtain information they desired. One congressman, who was having difficulty in deciding on the issues, complained that no one came to his office to contact him; only when he sought them out had he seen lobbyists. "To many congressmen," conclude Bauer and his associates, "the interest organization is a source of information about the attitudes of significant groups in his public, a source of research data and speech material, and an unofficial propaganda ally to help him put his case forward."[4]

\In the eyes of both state and national legislators, then, interest groups perform functions—representational, service, and political assistance—that legislators consider valuable.\ Interest groups try to influence policy in legislatures, many of whose principal actors see themselves as brokers and adjusters among such groups. Legislators often have a wide area of freedom regarding public policy and considerable discretion to act on issues. In such an environment, the fact that the legislative orientation is, on the whole, permissive and that interest group activity is assessed by legislators as aiding them affords such groups opportunities for pushing their own claims in the most advantageous manner.

Lobbyists and Lobbying: The Direct Approach to the Legislature

\ Lobbyists are responsible to their interest groups in a variety of ways. At the minimum, they act solely as passive intermediaries between legislative decision makers and their interest groups.\Only a few occupy themselves in this manner, however, serving as listening posts, passing on information regarding legislative actions or inten-

---

[3] Raymond A. Bauer, Ithiel de Sola Pool, and Lewis A. Dexter, *American Business and Public Policy, The Politics of Foreign Trade,* Atherton Press, New York, 1963, pp. 433–34.

[4] *Ibid.,* pp. 440–41.

tions relevant to their groups. The majority are also advocates who seek to advance or defend the positions and goals of their groups within the government. Since the American legislature is a central locus for making policy and for influencing the creation, interpretation, and implementation of policy in the executive and the judiciary as well as at the various levels of the federal system, the large number of lobbyists are active in the legislature. As actors more or less intimately involved in the legislative process with those who make authoritative decisions, they have available a number of strategies and tactics. At the same time, they must play by the "rules of the game" or pay severe penalties.

Direct lobbying, in which interest group representatives visit and speak with legislators personally, remains the primary strategy upon which most groups rely to influence legislative action. Although it is often inadequate and has increasingly given way in priority and effectiveness to indirect lobbying, the latter is frequently based in part upon the skills involved in direct lobbying and information collected thereby. Approximately 80 per cent of a sample of Washington lobbyists studied by Lester W. Milbrath responded that they preferred the direct method in trying to persuade a member of the Congress to their point of view.[5] Milbrath suggests that this preference for personal contact may stem from the fact that only lobbyists for large and affluent groups can effectively use the indirect method. Even such lobbyists, however, combine the two approaches.

It is significant that lobbyists and the congressmen with whom they must interact gave strikingly similar ratings to three types of direct lobbying tactics. On an effectiveness scale from 0 to 10 for rating what brings home better a point to a governmental official, over 58 per cent of Milbrath's Washington lobbyists and 52 per cent of his congressional respondents rated at ten (most effective) the "personal presentation of viewpoints"; 69 per cent in a study of Michigan lobbyists agreed.[6] The higher ratings by the state lobbyists were attributed to their probably easier access to state legislators. "The presentation of research results" was not rated as high, and testifying before legislative committees was graded lowest by all three groups. Nevertheless, a committee hearing presents an opportunity for an interest group to establish a public record for subsequent debate and national publicity. At times, moreover, the hearing becomes a factor in determining whether the committee moves the bill on at all.

[5] Lester W. Milbrath, *The Washington Lobbyists*, Rand McNally & Co., Chicago, 1963, p. 212.
[6] *Ibid.*, p. 213.

Lobbyists and Legislators: Personal Relations

Certain "rules of the game" prevail among lobbyists and legislators regarding appropriate lobbying. Both sets of actors hold similar views on this matter. Hence, these rules represent accepted norms whose violation can invoke legislative sanctions.

(A) THE LOBBYIST MUST BE TRUSTWORTHY   A lobbyist must be trustworthy and reliable or else the legislator will deny him access. Trust is the *sine qua non* for the lobbyist-legislator relationship. This writer recalls a United States senator making this point in explaining why he had discontinued all contact with a departmental legislative liaison officer during the Eisenhower Administration. This "executive lobbyist" had promised the legislator he would pursue a specific course of action, and the senator, then a House member, had acted on that premise. When the liaison officer failed to carry out his promise, the congressman ceased thereafter to trust him. Both executive lobbyists and congressmen emphasized to this writer, in 1962–63, the importance they assigned to honesty and reliability on the part of lobbyists in maintaining relationships of trust and confidence with legislators. Milbrath's study also stresses honesty as a critical aspect of a lobbyist's entree and effectiveness in the legislative system.

The legislative system operates in such a manner that no one individual has absolute power, knowledge, or independence. Moreover, legislators are vulnerable to their colleagues, the press, and the voters. All the actors must depend to a certain extent upon others, and this dependency is manifested in the rules inherent in a system of trust. The lobbyist must work, therefore, toward developing a trust-type of relationship which involves his demonstrating such traits as honesty, dependability, sincerity, respect for one's sources, and a willingness to provide information and services when called upon. One major mistake in this respect on the part of the lobbyist destroys not only any future relations with a legislator, but also imperils the lobbyist's reputation within the legislative subsystems and informal groups of which the legislator is a member.

(B) LOBBYISTS MUST NOT EMPLOY THREATS   The use of threats is resisted by legislators and can often prove dysfunctional to the interest group. Bauer and associates concluded that vigorous representation by interest groups in the politics of the Reciprocal Trade Agreements Acts of 1953–55 was perfectly acceptable as long as it did not involve threats![7] Threats were not considered legitimate

[7] Bauer *et al., op. cit.,* p. 434.

in the legislators' frame of reference, and they reacted antagonistically to them.

Commenting upon the lack of finesse exhibited by labor delegations in threatening congressmen during face-to-face lobbying relations at the time of the fight for the Full Employment Bill of 1946, Stephen K. Bailey notes: "Unless there is a reasonable chance that a pressure delegation can deliver on its threats, the use of threatening language does little except to stiffen the resistance of the Congressman."[8] Possibly, if a legislator were dependent upon an interest group, which through money or votes could affect his nomination or reelection, he could be threatened with relative impunity. But relatively few groups possess sufficient leverage over legislators on the national scene. However, the politics invoked in the California state legislature, in the period 1930–50, and to some extent today, would indicate that state legislators were more vulnerable to threats.

House and Senate members who commented to this writer on their relations with lobbyists from the executive establishment vehemently asserted that threats were intolerable and unacceptable. During the Kennedy Administration some executive lobbyists did resort to threats of one sort or another—or so some congressmen interpreted their lobbying at times. The congressional reaction revealed a general hostility to this style and indicated that it was on the whole ineffective. The major executive lobbyists, cognizant of this situation, contended that to threaten a congressman, even when the executive had the type of power to carry it through, was not only improper but dangerous.

Legislators have a strong sense of their own importance and integrity. Milbrath reports congressmen and lobbyists in agreement that when the latter do threaten to withhold a political contribution, should congressmen not cooperate, such threats are totally ineffective. In fact, this type of behavior is likely to result in reprisals against the lobbyist rather than acts of cooperation by the legislator. On the other hand, contributions to campaign funds are welcome and are extremely useful in providing access for interest groups. They may not changes votes very often, but they certainly afford lobbyists more sympathetic audiences.

It must be stressed here, in view of commonly held notions that legislators can be influenced by lobbyists' threats or money, that most legislators have a wide degree of latitude as to how they may act on legislation. Very few interest groups are dominant or hold the bal-

8 Stephen K. Bailey, *Congress Makes A Law, The Story Behind the Employment Act of 1946,* Columbia University Press, New York, 1950, p. 96.

ance of power in legislative constituencies. Even when they are powerful, they may be disinterested in the vast range of legislative issues. Groups want the support and cooperation of legislators on a variety of issues over a period of time; a fatal break with a legislator at any point can endanger their relations regarding other issues of concern to them in the legislative process. As for the voters in the constituencies, very few are conscious of, or follow, their legislators' actions on most issues.

It has been argued with considerable justification that the more interest groups there are seeking to influence a legislator, the freer he is to vote and act. In such cases, threats by any one interest group can be ignored, repudiated, or punished with ease. In the legislative process, the interest group more often is in greater need of the legislator than he of it.

(C) BRIBERY IS AN INEFFECTIVE LOBBYING TACTIC   Bribery is rejected by lobbyists and congressmen alike as being ineffective as well as inappropriate. It is also a most risky tactic, which can rebound to the great disadvantage of the user. Yet folklore, based upon an earlier historical era of loose political and business morality, conveys an impression of considerable bribing of legislators by lobbyists. That some bribery persists is true—although probably more at the state level than in the Congress. Several congressmen who had served in different state legislatures reported to Milbrath that bribery was more characteristic of state legislatures. "It does happen fairly often . . . before state legislatures," was one comment.[9]

Direct bribery is simply not a significant element in the influence pattern at the nation's capital. Milbrath reported a consensus among all the actors involved—lobbyists, congressmen, legislative staffs— that, with rare exceptions, congressmen are not bribable. Bribery is all the more hazardous in view of the alertness of a first-class Washington press corps and the readiness of the opposition party and other groups to capitalize upon such incidents.

An alleged bribery incident that occurred during the gas and oil industries' campaign in behalf of the Natural Gas Bill of 1956 is a perfect example of the fatality of such tactics. After the bill had narrowly passed the House of Representatives, backed by an effective lobbying campaign, its passage in the Senate appeared imminent. At this time, one oil company, on its own initiative, employed a lobbyist who, in seeking to advance the passage of the bill, made financial contributions to certain *favorable* Republican senators or their local

[9] Milbrath, *op. cit.*, p. 277.

parties. One such senator repudiated the contribution and charged publicly on the floor of the Senate that it represented a bribe. He announced that he would change his vote and oppose the bill. Although the Senate passed the bill in spite of this scandal, the President vetoed it.

President Eisenhower, who supported the principles of the bill and would probably have signed it with enthusiasm, vetoed it because of what he called "arrogant lobbying." Despite the massive lobby of the gas and oil companies and their allies, the expensive public relations campaign (it cost them over $1,500,000), passage through Congress and a favorably disposed President, a single $2,500 contribution by one lobbyist frustrated all their efforts. A Senate investigating committee subsequently labeled the contribution a "manifestly improper" attempt to influence the Senate but not an "illegal" one.[10]

In 1958, this legislation suffered a somewhat similar fate, again from the linking of oil money to its passage. In a letter soliciting contributions for a fund-raising dinner to honor the Republican leader of the U.S. House of Representatives, the Texas Republican national committeeman urged oil men to contribute because a large fund was needed to make certain that the bill would pass the Congress. The ensuing national publicity proved fatal to the bill; it was never brought to the floor in either chamber.

(D) THE "SOCIAL LOBBY" IS PERMISSIBLE   It is considered within the bounds of propriety for lobbyists to wine, dine, and entertain legislators. If one could rely upon popular myth, this is where lobbyists really twist legislators around their fingers. However, such tactics are judged by both lobbyists and national legislators as probably the least effective of them all.

Charles L. Clapp reports that a substantial proportion of congressmen consider attendance at breakfasts and dinners sponsored by interest groups as among the least appealing aspects of their jobs.[11] Unless constituents will be present, many congressmen do not accept such invitations. They regard social lobbying as a bore and an inconvenience. The lobbyists and congressmen whom Milbrath interviewed also attached little or no importance to entertainment tactics or to gifts. Nevertheless, some lobbyists consider entertainment worthwhile in helping to keep open communications between themselves and legislators.

[10] Edith T. Carper, *Lobbying and the Natural Gas Bill,* Inter-University Case Program, No. 72, New York, 1962, p. 38.

[11] Charles L. Clapp, *The Congressman, His Work As He Sees It,* The Brookings Institution, Washington, D.C., 1963, p. 170.

State lobbyists place a higher premium upon social lobbying. Michigan lobbyists rated it higher and spent considerably more time at it than did Washington lobbyists.[12] Unlike many congressmen who establish a second home in Washington, state legislators tend to reside in hotels at their state capitals and, therefore, are more accessible to lobbyists. In a large number of states without legislative office chambers, the working office of the legislator is his hotel room. In immediate proximity are the hotel rooms and offices of the lobbyists. The opportunities for their meeting and interacting, professionally and socially, are enhanced under such circumstances. Lobbyists can more easily pick up the bill for all of a legislator's meals, and they are in a position also to provide more lavish entertainment. The study of California legislators indicated that this worked to the decided advantage of the lobbyists.

(E) LOBBYISTS AND LEGISLATORS AS FRIENDS, NEUTRALS, AND OPPONENTS   Aside from the lobbyists for a very few interest groups —the League of Women Voters and the AFL-CIO—most do not attempt to contact those whom they consider to be their legislative opponents. Milbrath's sample of lobbyists reported that for them to do so was a painful personal experience as well as a waste of time. Some of his congressional respondents also stressed that lobbyists were least effective when they urged upon a member what he opposed. Since both sets of actors seem to agree on the inapplicability of this tactic, and in view of the fact that many lobbyists are generally overworked and command only limited resources, the latter feel that they cannot afford to spend their time on the opposition.

Most direct lobbying is aimed, therefore, at activating the converted, convincing the neutrals, or working with those members of the legislature who are wavering. An attempt to persuade a legislator who is opposed to the interest group's proposals risks engendering bad feelings on his part and straining whatever bonds of trust exist between lobbyist and member. If no trust relationship exists in the first place, personal contact by the lobbyist to change votes is virtually an exercise in stupidity as well as futility. Legislators can easily impose sanctions, ranging from a refusal to listen or discuss matters to attacks upon the lobbyists on the floor of the chamber. In extreme cases, legislators may succeed in denying or withdrawing from representatives of interest groups the right to operate as lobbyists.[13]

[12] Milbrath, *op. cit.,* p. 277.
[13] Samuel C. Patterson, "The Role of the Lobbyist: The Case of Oklahoma," *The Journal of Politics,* Vol. 25, No. 1, February, 1963, p. 74.

Most of the lobbyists involved in the controversy over the Natural Gas Bill of 1956 avoided any attempt to convince their opponents. When the Council of Local Gas Companies set up a lobby to oppose this bill, its leaders deliberately disregarded those senators whom they thought might reasonably favor the bill because "they come from producing States, and I thought it would be a waste of time. . . ."[14] These lobbyists did contact senators known to be opposed to the bill and also those whom they estimated might vote properly because their states consumed more gas than they produced. It was assumed that such legislators should, therefore, have an interest in their side. On the other hand, lobbyists for the United Automobile Workers' Union, who campaigned actively against the bill, called personally on senators already recorded as favoring the bill. These contacts proved fruitless. One such visit to a senator normally sympathetic to labor was reported to have lasted a full five minutes. The legislator's mind was made up, and he was publicly committed.

This disposition to avoid legislative opponents seems to have become part of the operational code of most lobbyists. That it handicaps needlessly the interest groups in putting together their strongest legislative force is a criticism advanced by Bauer, Pool, and Dexter.[15] These critics contend that interest groups and their lobbyists thereby frequently miss opportunities to split the opposition by arranging compromises with those who might be willing to adjust their positions if certain of their objections were overcome. The critics concede that it is reasonable to avoid outspoken opponents—those acting as spokesman for the other side. But they point out, regarding the lobbyists involved in the reciprocal trade politics of 1953–55, "we observed no more common mistake than failing to push people who were movable because it was assumed that they were on the other side."[16]

Although this criticism has some merit, it is nullified in part by the fact that lobbyists often rely upon others to contact opponents: constituents, friends, or lobbyists whose access is considered more legitimate. In the 1962 fight on reciprocal trade, liberal trade groups did apply more pressure on those opposing the bill. In contrast with the campaigns of 1953–55, the President was personally committed to his free trade bill. John F. Kennedy designated it the number one item on his legislative agenda, and he threw the entire weight of the White House and the executive establishment into the fight. Although

---

14 Carper, *op. cit.,* p. 34.
15 Bauer *et al., op. cit.,* pp. 350–53.
16 *Ibid.,* p. 351.

they failed in their efforts to bring the chemical industry behind the bill, the liberal-trade leaders successfully approached the textile industry which had previously opposed it. Only the President as "chief executive" and "chief legislator" could have promised the textile industry the executive and legislative actions necessary to satisfy the self-interest of this group and to weld it into the coalition behind this bill. It is extremely doubtful whether this feat could have been accomplished by the lobbyists themselves or even by the official leaders of the interest groups favoring reciprocal trade legislation.

Lobbyists, Interest Groups, and Other Lobbyists

There are lobbyists and then there are lobbyists. Some are effective; others are not. They bring a variety of experiences to their jobs. Among Milbrath's sample of Washington lobbyists for private groups, interestingly enough, very few, only three out of 114, had ever served as members of the Congress. In fact, the overwhelming majority had no previous experience in Congress, coming principally from the executive side of government and from business. Few were active in political parties; almost 50 per cent had never been active. In comparison, the "lobbyists" for the executive departments and the White House in Washington had, with very few exceptions, worked previously on the Hill. And the overwhelming majority had been very active in party affairs.

(A) LOBBYISTS AND INTEREST GROUPS   Not only do trade association executives often register as lobbyists, but the heads of individual business firms that belong to such associations also engage in lobbying. Both may employ full-time lobbying staffs of their own or hire the services of legal firms, public relations agencies, or special lobbyists to deal with the legislature.

Milbrath points out that most trade association executives dislike lobbying. In fact, they prefer to contact the executive branch rather than the legislature. But businessmen who are members of such trade associations seem to look down their noses at the executives of their own associations.[17] Just as businessmen have little confidence in the abilities of their associational representatives, so do the latter and their staff lobbyists tend to feel that their clients are naive, unsophisticated, and unrealistic about approaching the Congress.[18]

Business leaders may bypass completely their regular business associational groups on major legislative campaigns. In the 1955–56 fight on the Natural Gas Bill, executives of the principal firms in the

17 *Ibid.,* p. 330.
18 *Ibid.,* pp. 330–31.

oil and gas industries did not rely at all upon the American Petroleum Institute with its staff of 360, which had previously been the principal spokesman for representing their interests to the government and for handling public relations. Instead, they established separate *ad hoc* units, one to lobby for the legislation and the other to influence public opinion.

Elected officers of trade unions may also register as lobbyists with the Congress. Milbrath found that their tenure of office was longer than that of trade association executives; they placed more emphasis upon grass roots activities; and they tended to be highly active in partisan politics. The latter trait differentiated them sharply from most Washington lobbyists.

The wealthier larger groups—Farmers' Union, U.S. Chamber of Commerce, U.S. Conference of Mayors, AFL-CIO, American Farm Bureau Federation, National Grange—have special staffs of full-time lobbyists. In a few cases, the size of these staffs permits a division of functions: some lobby with the legislature and others with the executive. Most, however, work with both branches of the national government. At the state level, lobbyists also tend to work with executives as well as legislators. On the other hand, many such lobbying operations are one-man affairs, which often represent various interest groups on part-time assignments.

At the national level even *ad hoc* lobbying units, if they are established by large, well-financed interest groups, can constitute an impressive combination of resources and staff. The oil-gas industries and their allies set up a smooth working, well-financed operation to lobby in 1955–56 for the Natural Gas Bill. One of their strongest opponents, the Council of Local Gas Companies, an *ad hoc* group, was also relatively well financed and staffed with engineers, economists, lawyers, and rate specialists from its member utility companies. The operational headquarters of this group in Washington was manned by key executives from these companies. It worked closely with senators leading the campaign against the bill, helping to draft amendments and lobbying other senators and their assistants.

Groups whose organizational headquarters lie outside the nation's capital often employ Washington representatives. The latter operate mostly smaller, one-man offices or, at times, one individual may represent several organized groups. Milbrath reported that the typical clients of such Washington representatives were churches and humanitarian groups, corporations, and small trade associations.

Two increasing types found to be operating in Washington are the "consultants" and the "entrepreneurs." The former are principally lawyers whose work is not chiefly devoted to lobbying but rather to legal practice before courts and commissions. To them, lobbying for a bill generally represents only another legal case. On the state level, legal firms are also hired to represent groups that have something at stake in the legislature. In North Carolina, in 1965, for example, the legal firm of which the chairman of the Democratic Party was a member was hired by the North Carolina Fisheries Association. Milbrath characterizes lobbyist "entrepreneurs" as either selling their expertise and reputations in a particular subject matter area to those who support their points of view or as acting as general contractors. On the basis of their special knowledge about the governmental scene and lobbying, the latter type are employed to work on particular issues, subcontracting aspects of their work—bill drafting, publicity and research—to others.

An additional type should be mentioned, which will be discussed later in terms of the executive, the liaison agents of the executive departments and the White House who function as their "lobbyists." Compared with most of the other Washington lobbyists, these executive "lobbyists" are involved much more frequently and more intensely in the legislative process. Their employers are the executive heads of the departments and the President. Those working for the departments are responsible for helping their secretaries move their legislative programs, for coordinating departmental activities in the Congress, and for protecting their positions there. The White House staff is similarly responsible for the President's program and seeks to coordinate the work of the departmental lobbies. The activities of all of them are similar to those of the lobbyists for the private interest groups and for the public or institutional groups of the other levels of the American system. However, as special assistants to the political heads of the departments and to the President, they have a somewhat different relationship with the Congress than do the private lobbyists. And since they are representatives of the incumbent administration, they are highly partisan, unlike the overwhelming majority of private lobbyists. At the same time, however, they, too, must observe the "rules of the game" and are faced with similar problems and challenges.

(B) OVERCOMING LIMITATIONS OF STAFF, FINANCES, AND OTHER RESOURCES Anticipating well-organized, adequately financed, and highly effective lobbying operations, the authors of the study on the politics of reciprocal trade were surprised by the contrast. "When we look at a typical lobby, we find that its opportunities for maneuver are sharply limited, its staff mediocre, and its major problem not the

influencing of Congressional votes but the finding of clients and con-
tributors to enable it to survive at all."[19] This study dealt only with
one issue, and, in particular, with business and trade associations
and specialized interest groups.

Milbrath's study confirms that much of lobbying in Washington
is performed by small staffs with inadequate personnel and skills to
engage simultaneously in the time-consuming job of watching for
legislation and actions affecting their groups and in lobbying effectively. Nevertheless, the present writer is familiar with small staff
lobbies that are considered effective and that are highly esteemed by
congressmen and fellow lobbyists alike.

Small interest groups can overcome limitations of money and staff
and, at the same time, take advantage of the resources of large-scale
organizations by uniting with other interest groups in special lobbying coalitions. Increasingly, this cooperative endeavor is becoming
characteristic of lobbying in Washington. United fronts or coalitions
among lobbyists offer advantages for large as well as small groups.
Congressman "X" may be more sympathetic to the small interest
group than to any of the larger ones in the coalition. Or the small
group's lobbyist can sometimes bring just the right constituent or
friend to talk with a key legislator. Tactically, the coalition affords
both small and large groups a division of labor so that each can
concentrate on particular legislators or segments of the legislature.
Lobbyists committed to a common cause in legislation can more
successfully engineer a grass roots campaign from a wider area.
Coalition lobbies serve, moreover, as important centers for the exchange of information and for the feeding of such data into common
strategy as well as tactics.

Congressmen find such united efforts advantageous from their
own point of view. It provides them with a more effective group of
allies and collaborators and a broader base for research. On whatever side of an issue a legislator finds himself, he prefers unity from
those groups associated with him; otherwise, he risks offending someone, or he may be faced with conflicting and confusing signals.

The National Housing Conference is one such coalition that provides leadership for a number of interest groups concerned with slum
clearance, urban renewal, and housing legislation. Founded in 1931
by a small group of civic and social leaders desiring to fight more
effectively against slums, it has had a hand in the passage of the
U.S. Housing Act of 1937, the basic statute for urban renewal and

[19] *Ibid.*, p. 324.

public housing, and in the passage as well as the provisions of subsequent housing acts.

The NHC serves as a clearing house on housing legislation for more than forty national groups: religious, labor, educational, welfare, women's, veterans', and a number of public governmental groups. It engages in educational campaigns, seeks to unite those who want to be active in housing, and concentrates on the enactment of legislation in the Congress. As distinct from its constituent groups, who employ their own lobbying staffs, the NHC does not utilize its staff to bring out the vote on the floor in Congress. Rather its staff works with the chairmen of the legislative committees and with certain influential members. The NHC attempts also to mobilize its member groups in the constituencies of legislators.

The Electric Consumers Information Committee, another permanent coalition of interest groups, is committed to the cause of public power and to the protection of the consumer. It does not, itself, engage in lobbying but acts as a unifying center for bringing together the lobbyists for the consumer-oriented, non-profit power groups. The committee emerged from a National Electrical Consumers Conference that brought together in 1952 a number of groups. In 1962, the ECIC had a small budget based on voluntary contributions and a full-time executive director. Among the fourteen national groups sponsoring it were the Cooperative League of the USA, the American Public Power Association, the National Farmers' Union, and the Industrial Union Department, AFL-CIO. Regional and state groups were primarily rural electrification associations, electric consumer associations, state cooperatives and farmers' groups, state municipal utility associations, and 172 local rural electric and public power systems.

Many collaborative enterprises are *ad hoc* affairs. They coalesce the efforts of a number of groups around a particular issue and then dissolve to form again on different issues. They may not have a full-time staff. A sympathetic legislator and his staff or one of the lobbyists from the participating groups may assume responsibility for coordinating policy, strategy, and tactics. The Lib-Lab Lobby, which sparked the fight for the Employment Act of 1946, was such an *ad hoc* group.

Increasingly, lobbyists in Washington are finding it profitable to belong to a number of *ad hoc* and permanent groups so that they can exploit the potential strength of these groups behind the variety of issues that concern them. More permanent organizations of such coalitions have crystallized around more or less permanent issues.

The civil rights groups, for example, have been integrating their policies and efforts on a much more sustained basis although they do not have a special separate staff for their common bloc; in 1965, fully seventy organized groups were reported to be cooperating in this fashion. A number of coalitions raise funds to employ their own staffs, some of whom engage in direct lobbying. But the more prevalent version of inter-lobbying cooperation is the coalition that coordinates strategy and tactics, shares information, and assigns to its members the tasks of lobbying and activating the grass roots.

Problems, Opportunities, and Strategies in Lobbying

Whether groups are marshaling pressure at all points of the legislative process, or their lobbyists are merely attempting to establish the proper rapport with legislators, they all confront certain problems and opportunities.

The Need for Access

Interest groups must have access to legislators, their staffs, committees, and to the party leadership, if possible. To provide the group with an opportunity for presenting its case is to afford it only the shallowest form of access. Most groups encounter little difficulty in obtaining this type of access since legislators recognize the legitimacy of group intervention in the legislative process. All things being equal, unless an interest group is considerably outside the boundaries of respectability, its representatives will generally find access to some members of the legislative system. Richard E. Neustadt relates the success of one individual, originally associated with no organized group, who with great persistence managed to peddle his proposal for special loans to veterans with enough House and Senate members to lay the foundation for a major legislative campaign.[20] Eventually an interest group sponsored his proposal and the Administration itself was compelled to deal seriously with it.

Access based upon a sympathetic attitude on the part of the legislator is much more useful, for it can determine whether the group's claims and its lobbyists are seen in the context of friends and allies or as outsiders invested with no special claim to privileged treatment. The tone of the relationship between the interest group and legislator is different when the group is considered merely one among a number

---

[20] Richard E. Neustadt, "Presidential Clearance of Legislation," unpublished doctoral dissertation, Columbia University, 1950, pp. 128–35.

of claimants for attention and when the legislator views the group
as a collaborator, a political force representing common ends, or
as a trustworthy source upon whom he can rely with confidence.
He and his staff then will be more likely to grant the group time,
effort, consideration, and extra special assistance. It is on this level
of access that interest groups function best in legislatures.

Interest groups, too, require a variety of services from legislators.
This mutuality of need makes for a reciprocal relationship. Lobbying
is not a one-way street. Lobbyists needs the benefit of the insight,
special information, legislative skills, and positions which the legislator possesses. In other words, the legislator possesses resources
which the interest group does not have and which, if it can marshal
in its behalf, are of tremendous value in advancing its cause. Moreover, the legislator may, at the minimum, be induced to serve as a
favorable adherent and, at the maximum, as a leader and active
collaborator in common legislative endeavors. Assistance and collaboration may include introducing legislation, guiding its progress or
impeding that of other groups in committee, cooperating in floor
fights, advising on strategy and tactics, helping to constitute or prevent
a quorum, intervening with the political executive or with the bureaucracy, collaborating with either or both of these sets of executive
actors, or collaborating with members of the other legislative chamber.

In the committee and at the end of the process voting becomes
critical to the interest group. Not all votes are vital to a legislator or
his party. Hence, he is relatively free to make whatever political
arrangements he wishes with interest groups. Although roll call votes
commit legislators, in most states and in Congress voting is more
frequently *viva voce* which does not publicly identify the legislator.
This, too, facilitates his cooperation with interest groups. In addition,
the groups may be satisfied with an understanding that the legislator
will not be present for a vote or to make up a quorum. And if the
outcome is assured, interest groups and legislators may agree in
advance that the latter will vote against the position of the group if
such a course will help the member in the legislature or with his
constituents.

Service and Political Collaboration

Since legislators want and need staff aid, interest groups seek
opportunities to supply such services. To the extent that they can,
they strengthen their reservoir of good will and their potential for
influence. At the same time, it must be understood that the providing
of services is in itself a means for directly affecting legislative policy.

In 1957, Senator Mike Monroney (Okla. D)˙induced Congress to express itself in favor of an independent aviation authority.[21] However, the Administration was moving very slowly, and both military and civilian aviation authorities were often at odds. Into this situation entered the American Transport Association whose board of directors had adopted a resolution favoring an independent agency to regulate the use of air space and safety. At the initiative of the ATA's president, a conference was arranged with the senator and his staff at which the interest group's representatives urged that the time was appropriate and that it was legislatively feasible to move toward an independent agency with comprehensive powers.

"Notification of ATA's new position was the first of the events which led Monroney to a position of leadership in the passage of the Federal Aviation Act of 1958."[22] After consulting members of the aviation industry, the senator reported to the interest group that the time was indeed ripe for a bill to be framed and requested it to prepare the bill.

Senator Monroney had no technical specialists to assign to this task. Nor were there personnel in the Senate Committee on Interstate and Foreign Commerce with the knowledge and time to act quickly. Only the American Transport Association had the experts and the time to furnish the immediate assistance which the legislator required. Its teams of experts prepared the original draft which served as the basis for a major conference on the bill in which the senator's staff, ATA representatives, and representatives of the Civil Aeronautics Agency participated. This conference led to the Monroney bill, which was introduced in the Senate and which in amended version ultimately became law. Through the senator's staff, the ATA obtained a voice in negotiations with the President's own staff on the nature of an acceptable bill.

In this case, the interest group aided the legislator in seizing the initiative on a major piece of legislation; leadership in such instances generally originates from the executive. At the same time, the ATA played a major role in the legislative process in a policy area of vital concern to its membership.

Bauer and associates' study of interest group politics centering on the Reciprocal Trade Agreements Acts of 1953–55 concludes that interest groups operate most effectively as "service bureaus" for congressmen who agree with them.[23] A high point of effectiveness

[21] Emmette S. Redford, *Congress Passes the Federal Aviation Act of 1958,* Inter-University Case Program No. 62, New York, 1961, p. 9.

[22] *Ibid.,* p. 10.

[23] Bauer *et al., op. cit.,* Chapter 24, "Pressure Group or Service Bureau?"

was attained by the Committee for a National Trade Policy, a free trade group, when it placed itself at the services of Senator Albert Gore (Tenn. D). The senator needed assistance in preparing a comprehensive speech with which to introduce a bill calling for a three-year extension of the Reciprocal Trade Agreements Act for which he sought bipartisan support. Since his own staff could not provide this service, it turned to those advocates who could.

As the outstanding spokesman for liberal trade, the CNTP saw an opportunity to move forcefully in behalf of its cause. Its staff worked with that of the senator and others in providing him with a four-hour speech which he delivered on the floor of the Senate. In addition, the interest group arranged for statements of support from the titular head of the Democratic Party, Adlai E. Stevenson; and it contacted a number of Senate Republicans in an effort to offset Democratic defections. The authors of the study point to the service relationship and communication focus of interest groups as constituting their most effective means for having any impact upon legislation.

The participation by interest groups in the legislative politics of the Employment Act of 1946 exemplifies a number of ways in which interest groups can be effective.[24] They can constitute a seminal source for policy recommendations in the legislative system. In cooperation with ambitious, powerful members in the legislative system, they can play particularly influential roles. In addition to furnishing extremely valuable staff assistance, they can be powerful political allies in providing the public underpinning and the political "savvy" without which controversial legislative campaigns have little chance of success.

The National Farmers' Union was the author of the proposal from which emerged the principal full employment bill. A representative of the Farmers' Union participated in the committee of legislative and executive assistants who drafted the bill under the direction of the subcommittee staff of Senator James E. Murray (Mont. D). Parts of this bill were subsequently adopted in the compromise that emerged from the Congress. The legislative staffs of the senators concerned with the bill could not themselves mobilize and unify the strength of its potential friends; this was a difficult, time-consuming task. In this effort they were greatly aided by the formation of a liberal strategy group, the "Lib-Lab Lobby," which included representatives from seventeen to nineteen sympathetic groups and which met weekly under the leadership of Senator Murray's chief assistant.

[24] Bailey, *op. cit.,* Chapter 4, "The Staff in Room 15A," and Chapter 5, "The Lib-Lab Lobby."

Group intervention in terms of aid and collaboration acquires an added significance if it affords the legislator an opportunity to fulfill those roles which he aspires to play. The legislator wishes to be reelected, to help his constituency, and to be respected and liked by his fellow legislators. He may also desire to be recognized as a "legislative type," one who can play a creative and significant role in the making of policy; and, of course, he wants a good public image. To that extent, he is vulnerable to approaches from lobbyists, for interest groups can help him realize many of these goals.

As an assistant to a Democratic congressman in 1953, the author was able to ascertain how valuable interest groups could be to an ambitious legislator. This representative was interested in proposing legislation that would be constructive, build for the future when his party assumed control, and, at the same time, prove politically rewarding. The congressman turned first to various interest groups and knowledgeable individuals for advice and ideas. Once he had decided upon a proposal, his assistant conferred with the legislative experts of a number of interest groups for their analyses and suggestions; on the basis of their advice, a bill was drafted and subsequently altered and strengthened. Collaboration with a Democratic senator led to the introduction of the bill in both houses. It was never adopted in the Republican-controlled Congress, but both legislators felt they had gained political mileage out of the press coverage; and the representative was convinced that he had initiated a responsible proposal for improving the readiness of the executive to meet economic emergencies. In the process, the reputation of the congressman as a "legislative type" was reinforced within his own party and in the eyes of the interest groups.

Collaboration between lobbyists and legislators is not always as dramatic as in these cases. The furnishing of research by lobbyists and the conveyance of information are probably the most usual day-to-day types of interaction. Both lobbyists and legislative staffs in Congress rate the presentation of research findings as an effective lobbying tactic although the legislators, themselves, do not assign it a comparable value.

In *The Washington Lobbyists,* Milbrath concludes that the most important service lobbyists and their congressional collaborators can "perform for each other is the mutual exchange of information."[25] In a complicated legislative system where many sets of actors are involved—legislators, lobbyists, executive agents, party leaders—

[25] Milbrath, *op. cit.,* p. 173.

reliable information is at a premium, and few individuals have or can obtain by themselves the information which they require. Both the lobbyists and the legislators have some data that is of importance to the other, and each uses the other to obtain the necessary information upon which they must act.

The Significance of the Legislative Committee

Probably the most important focal point in the legislative process for interest groups is the committee. What it recommends is generally adopted by the legislature. In the Congress what is opposed in the legislative committees almost invariably dies there, and that which is moved on for consideration by the entire chamber may be radically altered in committee. Even in those state legislatures where bills must be reported out, the committee can be an important center of power. Influencing legislative decisions from outside the committee rather than from within is a much more difficult task for an interest group.

Proponents of federal aid to education for years found that the Senate Committee on Labor and Public Welfare was an extremely congenial locus of power.[26] They were able to secure hearings whenever they wished, and the committee reported bills favorably with bipartisan majorities. Commencing with 1948, the Senate passed general federal aid to education legislation each time it was considered.

The House Committee on Education and Labor on the other hand was a real stumbling block for those interest groups favoring federal aid to education. This committee refused to hold hearings or failed to report such bills over one half of the time in the seventeen year period preceding 1961. For a number of years prior to 1964, its chairman, a skillful tactician, was bitterly opposed to federal aid to education. When the committee did approve this legislation, its bills were stopped at later points in the legislative process, for reasons partially ascribable to the committee, itself. A bitterly divided committee, its views carried little weight in the House as a whole; and most of the bills it reported out were completely altered on the floor.

The legislative strategy of those favoring a higher minimum wage in 1955 was determined largely by their facing a hostile Committee on Education and Labor in the House.[27] Its chairman, who was

---

[26] Frank J. Munger and Richard F. Fenno, Jr., *National Politics and Federal Aid to Education,* Syracuse University Press, Syracuse, 1962, pp. 107–19.

[27] Gus Tyler, *A Legislative Campaign for a Federal Minimum Wage, 1955,* Eagleton Institute Case in Practical Politics, No. 4, McGraw-Hill Book Co., New York, 1960, pp. 5 *ff.*

publicly committed against minimum wage legislation, was strongly entrenched in his committee and worked closely with the minority party. Strategy was devised by the pro-minimum wage interest groups and their allies to move initially in the Senate where the committee was more favorable. Passage of such legislation in the Senate, plus the build-up of a massive campaign from the constituencies, was designed to exert sufficient pressure upon the House and its labor committee— to compel the latter to reconsider the bill. In the end, the Democrats on the committee were subjected to such pressure that they revolted against their chairman, and he was compelled to agree to hearings.

Even a favorable committee does not guarantee an interest group that its legislation will emerge in the form it desires especially if its bill is controversial in nature. Both the House and Senate committees that considered the oil and gas lobby's bill restricting the FPC's power over natural gas were sympathetic to the claims of the natural gas and oil industries. In fact, the chairman of the House committee had himself introduced the bill. Nevertheless, when it emerged from his committee, it contained a number of compromises that the committee had adopted in responding to the consumer-oriented forces who opposed the bill. Despite their keen disappointment, the leaders of the oil and gas lobby felt compelled to accept the bill; to have campaigned in the House against any part of the bill that the committee and its respected chairman had endorsed might have antagonized the latter, divided their own legislative sympathizers, and worked to the advantage of their opponents.

The very composition of a legislative committee may become an issue of bitter conflict among interest groups, so much is at stake. The long-time pre-eminence of the Rules Committee in the U.S. House of Representatives has made it a particularly strategic center of power. An almost unsurmountable obstacle to liberal-labor legislation has often been fashioned by conservative Democrats and Republicans on this committee. Consequently, when President Kennedy, the House Democratic leadership, liberal legislators, and their interest group allies sought to guarantee a more amenable majority on this committee, a number of the major interest groups involved themselves in these controversies, in 1961 and 1963. Those, like the Farm Bureau and the AMA, who wanted to preserve the old conservative majority, exerted pressure on legislators to upset this move whereas liberal and labor oriented interest groups actively solicited votes and built up support behind the Rules Committee change. A liberal-sponsored move, in 1965, to limit the power of the Rules Committee, which the House Democratic leadership accepted, brought many of these interest groups again into the legislative battle over this committee. The House leadership and its allied groups ultimately prevailed.

Timing

Timing is a critical element in any endeavor—and particularly so in legislative bodies. It is imperative that lobbyists be sensitive to the mood of the legislature, to the shifting configuration of political forces. In fact, one criterion by which lobbyists and legislators appraise the performance of those who lobby is their ability to sense when it is appropriate to delay and when to move, at what point and in what direction. Lobbyists for private interest groups, who, at this writer's solicitation in 1963, assessed the relative effectiveness of executive lobbyists, agreed that one reason "X" was effective was because he knew when to utilize them; and "Y" was ineffective because he focused them into the legislative process on his bills at the wrong time.

From his study of private lobbyists in Washington, D.C., Milbrath concludes that: "Timing is one of the main reasons that knowledge of the legislative and political process is so important for lobbying."[28] Lobbyists, themselves, assert that pushing for action at the wrong stage of the legislative process wastes a great deal of effort. To ask legislators and allied lobbyists to engage in futile maneuvers is to risk drying up future sources of support. Timing may often be more decisive for the fate of a bill than any other factor.

Failure to assess the changing mood of a legislative body can seriously nullify the efforts of an interest group. Operating on a false assumption of the possible, its lobbyists may never be attuned to the necessities of the moment and the possibilities of the future. Hence, their efforts lack flexibility and adaptability and prove self-defeating. In the controversy within the U.S. House of Representatives over what became the Labor-Management Reporting and Disclosure Act of 1959, the labor unions fell victim to their own lack of perceptiveness regarding legislative politics.[29]

A special Senate investigating committee, in 1957, had uncovered evidence of corruption and malpractice in a number of trade unions. In 1958, the Senate passed the Kennedy-Ives labor bill, which was designed to correct these abuses and to accommodate some of the

---

[28] Milbrath, *op. cit.,* p. 218.
[29] Sar A. Levitan and J. Joseph Loewenberg, "The Politics and Provisions of the Landrum-Griffin Act," in Marten S. Estey, *et al.,* eds., *Regulating Union Government,* Harper & Row, Publishers, New York, 1964, pp. 28–64.

unions' complaints against the Taft-Hartley Act. When the bill came to the House of Representatives, labor union leaders seemed to have miscalculated in their assessment of the Congress. The national AFL-CIO exerted only minimum pressure to secure the adoption of the Kennedy-Ives bill; the labor leaders had other priorities. With employer groups adamantly opposing the bill and labor disinterested or opposed, the bill failed. By not moving aggressively behind a bill that combined an attack upon improper union government and practices with a resolution of some union grievances against the Taft-Hartley Act, labor spokesmen forfeited the opportunity to obtain labor reform which benefited them. And by not acting when conditions for moderate legislation were still propitious, they permitted the fight over labor legislation to occur at a time when the House had become hostile to labor and on an even more vital issue.

In 1959, the AFL-CIO withdrew its support from an amended Kennedy-Ervin bill that the Senate had adopted and that again sought to enact labor reforms and meet union objections to the Taft-Hartley law. An even more favorable bill to labor reported by the House Committee on Education and Labor failed to elicit any support from AFL-CIO spokesmen. Employer groups skillfully seized the initiative to divert the legislature's concern away from an emphasis upon internal union government to a limitation upon labor's economic powers in management-labor relations. As a consequence, labor was confronted with two extremely restrictive measures, the Landrum and the Griffin bills, to which President Eisenhower gave his endorsement and support and behind which there developed considerable sentiment.

Afforded an opportunity to support the more favorable bill that the House Democratic leaders sponsored, labor's leaders refused to endorse it. As a result, labor's legislative allies had no bill around which they could rally. A strong pro-labor bill was subsequently introduced by a union legislator; but Democratic legislative leaders, traditionally sympathetic to labor's aspirations, were already committed to their own bill. Moreover, the mood of Congress was shifting increasingly in favor of tighter restrictions upon unions.

When the crucial votes were cast, it was clear that by insisting upon a rigid position in the face of a changing political climate, labor's leaders had locked themselves out of any possibility of backing an acceptable bill in the House. Instead, the very restrictive Landrum-Griffin bill, endorsed by conservative business and agriculture groups, was adopted. Not only had a number of COPE-supported legislators voted for the bill but labor's inflexibility had alienated other congressmen usually considered friendly to its cause. In the conference committee, the Senate's position in favor of more moderate legislation was further undercut by threats from a AFL-CIO vice-president to take reprisals in the 1960 elections against all congressmen voting for the Landrum-Griffin bill.

On the whole, the labor leaders never fully comprehended that a critical shift away from concern with internal union affairs had occurred in the House. Legislative attention had become focused on matters affecting management-union relations, but labor leaders and their lobbyists failed to adjust to the new circumstances. When they did engage in tactical retreats, invariably their timing was off. A bill which labor vehemently opposed was enacted into law.

Unity and Compromise

Labor's defeat on the Landrum-Griffin bill also demonstrates the importance of unity and compromise to interest groups which engage in legislative lobbying. When those who purport to speak for a common sector of society are divided, their legislative supporters are left confused and uncertain in which direction to turn. Moreover, they become irritated and resentful if they are unable to play any meaningful role, especially if compromise is rejected, and they are asked to oppose their party leaders. Damned if they do and damned if they do not by spokesmen from the same set of interest groups, they lose their ability to operate effectively for these groups because the latter fail to provide a sense of direction, and the legislators cannot capitalize upon the legislative system's preference for compromise and flexibility.

In 1959, the AFL-CIO had refused to support either a sympathetic Kennedy-Ervin bill or the more favorable Elliott bill that the House Education and Labor Committee had recommended. The Teamsters and the United Mine Workers fought both bills because they were opposed to any government regulation of labor unions. Only at the last minute did the AFL-CIO and the Teamsters join together for a bill that, however, was not supported by the Democratic leadership and, it was generally agreed, had little chance to pass. Once this bill was defeated, labor's friends in the Congress were confronted with the alternative of supporting a Democratic-sponsored bill that labor spokesmen opposed or the Landrum-Griffin bill with which business groups were closely identified.

Interest groups that make up what is loosely called the education lobby have been penalized in the past by an absence of unity in approaching the national legislature. The National Education Association and the American Federation of Teachers, for example, have encountered difficulties in cooperating on federal aid for education and have often proposed different legislation. In 1947, Senator Robert A. Taft pointedly took both groups to task, charging that the principal dangers to a bill for federal aid to education lay in the differences between its principal advocates.

On the other hand, a unified stance on legislation may be recognized as so vital to the long-range future of interest groups that they will at times agree to short-term, undesirable compromises in order to operate effectively in a legislature. The General Gas Committee, which planned and coordinated the oil and gas lobbying behind the Natural Gas Bill, successfully resolved its internal differences in the interests of limiting the powers of the Federal Power Commission. An *ad hoc* group, it was composed of 667 members representing various firms in the oil and gas industries as well as other business and industrial groups. The bill that the sympathetic chairman of the House Interstate and Foreign Commerce Committee introduced almost unhinged this coalition. The bill allowed pipeline producers to pass along only a "reasonable market price," which the FPC was empowered to determine, plus a "fair gathering charge." This created a split between the pipeline companies that also produced gas and the independent gas producers who wanted to free themselves but still keep the pipeline companies under FPC control.

The chairman of the General Gas Committee found that his principal task was to secure harmony between the pipeline companies and the independent producers. This course was deemed necessary in order to "present to this Congress an intelligent, solid front for all producers of natural gas. . . ."[30] Initially, he was able to convince the independent producers but not the pipeline companies of the propriety of some FPC regulation. Without such a compromise, the GGC leaders felt that congressmen from the coal states could not be kept in line behind the bill since coal industry spokesmen charged that pipeline gas was being sold at "dump" prices below that of coal.

The GGC leaders were convinced that they might lose if various parts of the coalition fought each other and campaigned for or against different parts of the same bill. Fortunately for them, the unity of their group was served by certain common fears among their members—that FPC regulation of the producer price of natural gas would next encompass oil and then coal, and that this constituted a serious threat to the whole free enterprise system. Under the compulsions

[30] Carper, *op. cit.*, p. 11.

of these sentiments plus the obvious tactical difficulty of attempting to lobby in the Congress when their component units were disputing among themselves, the leaders of the GGC ultimately secured undivided support behind the committee chairman's bill.

Identification With Key Legislative Leaders

Support from legislators occupying key party or committee positions strengthens the position of interest groups in the legislative system. Consequently, careful thought and effort are invested in a search for allies, often to the point of accepting otherwise unpalatable compromises or of modifying a bill to attract such support. The sponsorship of the Natural Gas Bill by Chairman Oren Harris and the wholehearted support by Speaker Sam Rayburn afforded the gas and oil lobby a tremendous advantage over its opponents. When to this combination was added the support of the majority leader of the Senate, the lobby was almost unbeatable.

By attracting legislative leaders to their side, interest groups can overcome much of the problem of rallying legislative support and repulsing attacks. On many issues legislators tend to accept the guidance of their fellow members who have earned respect as substantive experts or as party or committee leaders. Senator Robert A. Taft's endorsement of federal aid to education ensured such bills almost guaranteed success in the Senate. Not only was he "Mr. Republican" but he was recognized as an expert in this field. As a member of the substantive committee, the floor leader of his party, and the acknowledged national spokesman for conservatism, his support removed much of the bitter ideological controversy that characterized House consideration of this issue. No member of the Education and Labor Committee in the House of Representatives was possessed of a comparable stature and respect.

"Lobbying at the Grass Roots": Supplement to and Substitute for Direct Negotiations With Legislators

In the 1950's, a special congressional investigating committee called attention to a significant shift in lobbying, a shift that had occurred only in the previous two decades. In contrast with the "well-established methods of direct contact" by lobbyists, reported the committee, "this new emphasis in pressure tactics might best be called 'lobbying at the grass roots.' "[31]

[31] U.S. Congress, House, Select Committee on Lobbying Activities, *General Interim Report*, 81:2, H. Rep. No. 3138, GPO, Washington, D.C., October 2, 1950, p. 29.

Lobbying at the grass roots assumes that legislators are particularly responsive to public opinion. Direct lobbying becomes much more effective when it is supported by an articulate public. Without it, noted the committee, direct lobbying—the personal contacting of legislators by lobbyists—tends to be ineffective except on narrow issues.

Indirect lobbying involves, then, recourse to constituents, other interest groups, and to public opinion media in order to influence legislators. Interest groups often resort to both types of strategies, but differ according to their resources as to whether they stress one, the other, or both. Milbrath reports that the smaller and poorer groups, those with more technical concerns, and those with little power at the polls concentrate on direct lobbying in approaching the Congress. The larger and richer interest groups utilize both strategies. They have the staff to contact legislators as well as to mobilize support in the constituencies, and they possess the finances to mount ambitious "grass roots" campaigns.

Recourse on the state level to direct or indirect lobbying is, however, sometimes merely a question of an interest group's making the most of its resources and opportunities. In their efforts, during 1949–52, to repeal legislative weight limits upon loads that trucks could carry, the Pennsylvania truckers relied primarily upon direct lobbying, while their opponents, the railroads, invested their money in a public relations campaign.[32] These strategies were dictated by basic considerations of position. The Pennsylvania Motor Truck Association established an impressive, well-financed lobbying organization in the state capital. Its appeal to legislators was based primarily upon its ability to mobilize rank-and-file-truckers in their local constituencies and to marshal its finances to affect the election of legislators. In 1950, for example, the PMTA collected from its members $76,000 that it distributed in roughly equal amounts to the Democratic and Republican parties. Local truckers were instructed to contribute money directly to local candidates. Moreover, PMTA members were mostly small businessmen who lived in communities throughout the state. They were, therefore, in a particularly advantageous position to exert influence from within their communities upon their state legislators.

A massive public relations campaign was conducted by the

---

[32] Andrew Hacker, "Pressure Politics in Pennsylvania: The Truckers vs. The Railroads," in Alan F. Westin, ed., *The Uses of Power, 7 Cases in American Politics,* Harcourt, Brace & World, Inc., New York, 1962, pp. 323–76.

Pennsylvania Railroad and its allies in the Eastern Railroads Presidents Conference. The Pennsylvania Railroad did not have a mass membership nor were its employees independent businessmen who exerted influence in their local communities. The railroad could neither pay its employees to help defray the campaign expenses of state legislators nor could it as a large corporation compete with the truckers' small businessmen image. Neither was it organized to conduct campaigns in the home constituencies of state legislators.

On the other hand, the railroads collectively had the financial resources to hire a high-powered publicity firm with an enviable record of preventing the passage of legislation. It was employed at an annual retainer of $75,000 plus the full costs of all advertisements and publicity and the operating expenses of the public relations staff assigned by the firm to this issue. In the first year of its operation, this firm received more than $274,000 from the railroads over and above its annual fee.

Indirect Lobbying Tactics

(A) LETTER WRITING   One grass roots tactic that interest groups may employ is the letter writing campaign. Legislators represent constituents who have the power to affect their reelection. By stimulating constituents to write to their legislators, interest groups hope to influence the latter by demonstrating that issues are of real concern to those whom they represent.

There is mixed evidence on how effective letter writing is as a tactic. The attitude of legislators, themselves, toward such campaigns is ambiguous. While Washington lobbyists interviewed by Milbrath varied widely in rating the effectiveness of letter writing, responses tended to be weighted in the lower scales; only seven ranked it highest in effectiveness, whereas twenty graded it zero. His sample of congressmen ranked letter writing even 'lower. And it was consistently ranked low by Michigan lobbyists.

Washington lobbyists differed somewhat in their rankings according to the size of their groups. Those with a small membership ranked letter writing low, while labor and agricultural interest groups, with their large rank-and-file membership, credited this tactic with more effectiveness. Even these large groups, however, find that they must exert considerable effort to launch a flood of mail, and then they are never certain that the constituents will write the personal, committed letter that the interest groups desire.

Very few legislators change their minds as a result of letter writing campaigns once they have committed themselves publicly or within the legislative system. And many vote their own convictions and their conceptions of the districts' interests. But more than a few legislators, it has been noted, view their mail as reflecting their constituencies, and feel, therefore, that they are taking a big step when they vote contrary to their mail.[33] Depending on the individual and how he defines his duties in terms of his district, some legislators are responsive to their mail. Dexter credits letters from their districts with helping to shift the votes of southern congressmen, who were traditionally free trade supporters, away from the reciprocal trade program in 1955.[34] On the other hand, such legislators were apparently not among those greatly committed to the issue. The present writer has noticed that when members of the North Carolina legislature are not particularly concerned about an issue, a heavy flow of mail from the constituency tends to affect their actions.

Form and mimeographed letters are not only ineffective but are sometimes offensive. Congressmen often dismiss such letters as inaccurate reflections of opinion in their constituencies and as the obvious product of interest group stimulation. Congressmen and their staffs can generally detect such stimulation even when it is not crude or obvious.

While they welcome mail favoring their own positions, and they may even request interest groups to stimulate a flood of mail, legislators know that only a very small fraction of their constituents ever write. They recognize also that their reelection is bound up with so many issues that there is generally little for them to fear if they should ignore the demands of an avalanche of letters. The very presence of mail becomes, however, a force impinging upon the attention of the legislator and his staff. They cannot afford completely to overlook the mail because it provides them with an index of constituent thinking even when they know it is unrepresentative. For many legislators, it is often the only clue they have as to what their constituents are thinking.

A massive letter writing campaign can have some impact upon the national legislature but rarely in terms of altering a member's position. Rather it elevates to a higher level of saliency the issues being pressed. Congressmen have only limited time to allocate to a variety of issues, and they receive signals from many sources; therefore it is no mean accomplishment for such a campaign to induce legislators

---

[33] Bauer *et al., op. cit.,* p. 438.
[34] Lewis A. Dexter, "The Representative and His District," in Robert L. Peabody and Nelson W. Polsby, eds., *New Perspectives on the House of Representatives,* Rand McNally & Co., Chicago, 1963, pp. 21–22.

to examine more closely the legislation being advanced. An undecided legislator may, indeed, permit himself to be influenced; certainly, if he is unconcerned about an issue, he will be more inclined to follow his mail if it represents an insistent force. Moreover, original letters of opinion do receive careful consideration by many national legislators, especially if they are sent by individuals of local prominence and/or power. It is generally the case, however, that congressmen hear more from those who agree with them, which, in itself, tends to bolster the positions adopted by the legislators.

If such letters activate the neutral to consider issues more carefully, help the undecided to make up their minds, or induce the committed to move more forcefully, then letter writing campaigns produce valuable political dividends. Such campaigns require considerable organized effort and the results are uncertain, but interest groups that can mobilize letters from constituents take advantage of this tactic to strengthen themselves in the legislature.

(B) PUBLIC RELATIONS CAMPAIGNS Public relations campaigns are much more expensive than letter writing campaigns. They, too, are difficult to control and their effects are equally uncertain. A number of the more ambitious, well-financed campaigns are credited by some writers with stopping particular pieces of legislation: The margarine manufacturers' drive to discontinue federal taxes on oleomargarine; the AMA's efforts to defeat President Truman's and President Kennedy's health insurance programs.[35] However, one must appraise such claims with great care. To attribute the defeat of legislation to one factor alone in the complex, multifaceted world of politics is to oversimplify tremendously. The major agricultural group that fought to retain the tax on oleomargarine had already become so disunited that it had virtually withdrawn from the battle. The first two medical bills of the Kennedy-Johnson administrations foundered, in the end, on the opposition in the House Ways and Means Committee; the votes for medicare simply did not exist. Although the initial bill was defeated in the Senate in 1963, the second passed in 1964; but neither came up for a vote in the House.

With President Lyndon B. Johnson's massive victory, in 1964, and key personnel changes on the Ways and Means Committee, passage of hospitalization insurance for the aged under the social security system was recognized as almost a certainty. The AMA, itself, evidenced signs of confusion and demoralization in the face of this inevitability, especially since the chairman of the Ways and Means

---

[35] Milbrath, *op. cit.*, p. 250.

Committee, who had been unwilling to endorse medicare before, predicted early in 1965 that his committee would now move on it. Although the AMA came up with its own bill, the Committee on Ways and Means recommended and the House adopted an expanded version of the Administration's original bill. Unless the political configuration of forces are correctly aligned, not even an expensive public relations campaign can change the outcome.

From 1949 to 1952, the AMA and its affiliates expended over $4.6 million to defeat President Truman's medical insurance proposals; the fee of its public relations firm alone was $325,000.[36] Although the Whitaker and Baxter firm, Campaigns, Inc., is often credited with a superb job of marshaling the doctors, molding public opinion, and rallying other organizations, it was obviously aided in its efforts by a united Republican Party and by the fact that the Democrats, themselves, were divided. Nevertheless, it must be conceded that if the organized medical group had not fought the medical proposals, the proposals might have been adopted during this period.

The public relations campaign of the Pennsylvania Railroad and its allies in their fight to prevent the repeal of the weight limit on trucks failed completely in the state legislature in 1951. Yet, their public relations firm, which had placed a staff of 160 employees on the project, conducted an extremely ambitious and skillful campaign to affect public opinion. It was based upon a two-fold strategy: An attack rather than a defense, and the mobilization of other significant interest groups against the truckers' bill. Included among these groups were the state CIO, the General Federation of Women's Clubs, the Auto Club, the State Grange, and the State Association of Township Supervisors. Numerous articles and pictures planted directly in the mass media and indirectly through these groups depicted trucks as dangerous road hogs, destructive to roads, costly to taxpayers.

This campaign did not induce the Pennsylvania legislature to kill the bill although it was undoubtedly one factor in the decision of the governor to veto it. A subsequent governor from the opposite political party reversed even this decision when the legislature readopted the bill.

Where the principal actors in the legislative system favor the aspirations of a particular interest group, a public relations campaign, coupled with a direct lobbying campaign, may prove particu-

[36] Stanley Kelly, Jr., *Professional Public Relations and Political Power,* The Johns Hopkins Press, Baltimore, 1956, Chapter 2, "Medical Economics and Doctor Politics."

larly valuable. The gas and oil industries, which had set up a General Gas Committee to coordinate direct lobbying for the Natural Gas Bill fight of 1955–56, also established a Natural Gas and Oil Resources Committee to "educate" the public. Composed of officers and employees of the oil and gas companies, its function was to create a favorable image of the industry and to produce a climate of opinion conducive to passage of the bill. This committee engaged a public relations firm and raised over $1,900,000, of which it spent $1,400,000 for advertising, publicity, field programs, films, and television aids. In addition, it won support from 120 interest groups in thirty-four states, including the American Cattleman's Association and the American Farm Bureau Federation. Meanwhile, the oil and gas companies, themselves, endeavored to enlist the support of their employees, stockholders, and customers behind the bill.

Their bill was introduced by the chairman of the substantive committee that considered it; the Speaker of the House of Representatives was favorable as was the Majority Leader of the Senate; and the bill coincided with proposals made by an advisory committee to the Republican President. In spite of this aggregation of legislative powers, the bill narrowly passed in the House of Representatives, 209–202. It is possible that the combined lobbying-public relations endeavor helped produce the critical margin of votes. The proponents certainly thought that their time, effort, and money were well spent because their victory was a difficult one, despite a division among their opponents, a number of whom entered into the legislative battle very late.

(C) CONSTITUENTS AND FRIENDS   By introducing constituents and friends of the legislator into the campaign on an individual or group basis, lobbyists try to apply the personal touch and the tailored approach. These they cannot command via mass letter writing or public relations tactics. The latter are often referred to by lobbyists as the "shot gun" approach. However, the "rifle" approach poses its own problems because constituents must be located who will phone or appear personally to talk with the legislator, and friends of the legislator must be induced to capitalize upon their friendship in behalf of the interest group. Nevertheless, both of these approaches are characterized by a directness and a personal relationship that make them particularly useful. They personalize the grass roots with a face or name that signifies something definite to the legislator.

Bauer, Pool, and Dexter found to their surprise that the lobbyists involved in reciprocal trade politics, in 1953–55, served less as personal influencers upon congressmen and more as nodes in a communications service network. They endeavored to bring businessmen and others into direct and indirect relations with the legislators, hoping thereby to affect legislative decision-making. In Milbrath's study, congressmen rated contacts by close friends very high and rated constituent contacts nearly as high. Washington lobbyists utilized the constituent technique more frequently than that of close friends, if only because friends are fewer in number and constituents are more easily mobilized. Michigan lobbyists, on the other hand, assigned a low ranking to the use of constituents as well as friends.

It is significant that the Washington lobbyists who ranked constituents the highest were those who had worked in the Congress or who served on a legislative relations staff of an interest group, that is to say, they were full-time legislative lobbyists rather than lawyers or public relations men who acted as part-time lobbyists. Clearly, an intimate experience with the complexities of the legislative system provides such lobbyists with a special insight into the legislators' frames of reference. The capability for factoring into the legislative system the particular friend, constituent, or political contributor in the home district was prized highly by the lobbyists whom the present author interviewed in 1962–63. It was with envy and admiration that one conservationist lobbyist spoke of an executive lobbyist who was far more familiar than he was with the hunting and fishing habits of congressmen and their families—data vital to the conservationists lobbying in Congress.

Most of the lobbyists whom Milbrath interviewed employed constituent contacts very carefully. They utilized this tactic more to gain access than to attempt to persuade the legislators. The select group of effective lobbyists whom the present author interviewed were as inclined to have the constituent or the friend present their case to the legislator as they were to use them to gain access for themselves. Union lobbyists, for example, had developed a technique of importing union constituents by the bus load, offering them a short course in lobbying and then sending them off to see their congressmen.

Summary

A combination of the direct and indirect approaches is most productive for lobbyists and their interest groups over the long run. There are some legislators whom lobbyists may easily approach, talk frankly with, and predict how they are going to vote. It would be a waste of time and effort to direct external resources to these legislators. On the other hand, lobbyists know that their personal intervention has no useful effect upon other legislators. It might even antagonize them. In such cases, lobbyists turn naturally to others who loom more significantly or more favorably in the legislator's world.

The point here is that the more effective lobbyists know when, where, and how such intervention should occur. They can pinpoint trouble spots in the legislature and the loci of power and influence. From what they know and learn about individual members and the legislative process, lobbyists can advise on the timing of this intervention and the approach it should take. Moreover, if a lobbyist is doing a proper job, he can sense when and by what means the interest group should alter its position in order to adjust realistically to political exigencies. Such knowledge must come from direct, front line engagement in the legislative process.

The Legislature Regulates Lobbying[37]

In the formal legal sense, Congress has adopted rules that purport to regulate lobbying. But on the informal operational level lobbying is permitted, encouraged, and accepted as legitimate as well as useful by legislators. The same generalization holds true among state legislatures that have also adopted laws regulating lobbying. The truth of the matter is that the laws themselves are either inadequately drafted, extremely limited in scope, or simply not enforced. In essence, legislators are either unwilling or disinclined to place severe restrictions on lobbying by private interest groups, individual citizens, or even institutional groups, those representing segments of public government, for example.

As far back as 1876, Congress had begun to require some lobbyists to register. In the 1930's, as a result of its investigation of lobbying by utility companies, Congress required lobbyists to register if they represented holding companies before the Congress, the Federal Power Commission, or the Securities and Exchange Commission. This requirement was subsequently expanded to include other specific groups of lobbyists. The Federal Regulation of Lobbying Act of 1946 is the present national law affecting lobbyists and the interest groups that support their intervention in the legislative

---

[37] An excellent study of state regulation of lobbying can be found in Edgar Lane, *Lobbying and the Law,* University of California Press, Berkeley, 1964. See also William J. Keefe and Morris S. Ogul, *The American Legislative Process, Congress, and the States,* Prentice-Hall, Inc., Englewood Cliffs, N.J., 1964, pp. 361–65, and Milbrath, *op. cit.,* pp. 316–23.

process. As is the case with most state laws, it aims at disclosing the identity of those who lobby the legislators and those who finance the lobbyists.

Anyone who is paid or collects money for the principal purpose of affecting the course of legislation must register with officials of the House of Representatives and the Senate. They must also report quarterly the following data: the names of their employers; their salaries, expenses, receipts; the articles or editorials they have caused to be published; the legislation they are employed to oppose or support. In addition, any person or group that raises or receives money for the principal purpose of influencing legislation must file data on such contributions and expenditures. Included, therein, must be the names and addresses of persons giving more than $500 as well as those to whom expenditures of $10 or more have been made. Those convicted of violating this law face penalties that range up to a $10,000 fine, a five-year prison term, and a three-year ban on additional lobbying.

In upholding the constitutionality of the national lobbying law, the U.S. Supreme Court defined its purpose as helping the elected representatives evaluate properly the pressures upon them. Congress, pointed out the Court, "wants only to know who is being hired, who is putting up the money, and how much."[38] On the other hand, the Court ruled that only those whose *principal* purpose it was to influence legislation need register and file statements. This has exempted any individual, firm, or group that merely appears before a congressman or a committee to express views on legislation. Many interest groups that do, in fact, lobby decline to register on the grounds that they are exempt because their funds are not spent for the principal purpose of defeating or aiding legislation. Furthermore, groups may ignore the law with impunity, for no specific agency is responsible for policing the act.

The Court also decided that the law's regulations applied only to those lobbyists and groups communicating *directly* with the Congress. Therefore, lobbying with the executive is excluded from regulation by the law, and so, too, is indirect lobbying to affect the legislative process—the stimulation of letter campaigns, the shaping of public opinion, and the activating of other groups. Even the main purposes which the Court ascribed to the act, disclosure and legislative knowledge, are very poorly realized. The morass of informational material is merely filed; no one is responsible for assembling, analyz-

[38] U.S. *v.* Harris *et al.,* 347 U.S. 612, 625 (1954).

ing, or publicizing it.[39] Hence, groups and lobbyists feel free to file such information as they deem appropriate in their reports.

This national lobbying law did serve as the basis for punishing the oil company and its lobbyist who attempted to give a "campaign contribution" to Senator Francis Case during legislative consideration of the Natural Gas Bill of 1955. Both were convicted for having failed to file under the act, the individual as a lobbyist and the company as an organization spending money to influence legislation under terms of the Lobbying Act. The company was fined $10,000, the lobbyist and his immediate employer, $2,500 each.

A special Senate investigating committee that studied the lobbying on the Natural Gas Bill considered suggestions for strengthening the law. It proposed broadening the coverage to include "indirect lobbying" and imposing criminal penalties for influencing the sending of false messages to Congress. More specific criteria were offered as a substitute for the "principal purpose" test, and the bill incorporating these proposals also authorized the Comptroller General to analyze the data filed by lobbying groups and to enforce its provisions. In spite of the recommendations of this committee, neither house took any action on the bill. It is possible, of course, that should a scandal of a similar or greater magnitude again occur, the Congress might resort to these proposals as a basis for additional legislation.

At the request of business interest groups and Washington lobbyists, Congress, in 1962, amended the tax ruling that denied the permissibility of deductions for expenditures for influencing the legislature and propagandizing the public. The tax law was rewritten to permit deductions, as business expenses, of expenditures incurred in appearing before legislative committees or in communicating with congressmen regarding legislation of "direct interest" to the taxpayer. A portion of the dues that members paid to any organized group and that was used for these purposes was also declared deductible. Such legislation would indicate further that the national legislators viewed lobbying as an integral, legitimate part of the operation of modern business and organized groups. Congress refused, however, to permit deductions for expenditures or contributions for such indirect lobbying as public education and propaganda campaigns to influence the public.

Approximately forty states have laws that pertain to the registration of lobbyists or that forbid certain types of lobbying. None is as sweep-

---

[39] On a quarterly basis, The *Congressional Record* lists the registrations and reports. The *Congressional Quarterly* periodically publishes a simple analysis of these reports.

ing as the Georgia constitution of 1877 that declared the practice of lobbying, itself, to be a crime. Some states outlaw contingent-fee lobbying, the practice whereby a lobbyist receives special compensation if he succeeds in accomplishing that objective for which he is employed. On the whole, however, state laws seek principally to disclose and publicize for the benefit of the legislators who the lobbyists are and what they do. In Oklahoma, for example, those who would lobby must register and request the permission of the state legislature. Upon the approval of a majority of the House of Representatives who are present and voting, the lobbyist receives an official identification card. Those who do not comply with these requirements may be excluded and banished from the chamber. Nevertheless, as is true with the national law, the administration and enforcement of state lobbying laws are very lax.

While neither state nor congressional laws prohibit lobbying by private interest groups, *per se,* Congress has adopted what on its face appears to be a prohibition against lobbying by executive officials of the national government. In 18 U.S. Code, Section 1913, Congress specifically prohibited the use of appropriated funds by executive officers or employees for any services or communications intended to influence a congressman regarding legislation or appropriations. Attached to it are also criminal penalties, a fine of not more than $500 or imprisonment for not more than a year or both, plus removal from office.

Nevertheless, bureau heads in the executive have traditionally played a role approximating that of the lobbyists.[40] And increasingly, since 1947 when legislative liaison officers were recommended as staff assistants to the departmental secretaries by the initial Hoover Commission, the political heads of the executive departments have controlled the lobbying efforts of their departments in the Congress.

Both Milbrath's study of Washington lobbyists and that of this author, who studied the activities of the legislative liaison agents of the departments, reveal that congressmen accept and respect the right of the political heads of the departments and their immediate assistants to lobby. "Like prohibition," reported one senior congressman, "it [the anti-executive lobbying law] is observed in the breach." Congressmen growl, at times, when the executive seems to be "twisting arms" in its search for votes, but little is done about it. As for the legislative liaison agents or "executive lobbyists" for the

[40] J. Leiper Freeman, *The Political Process: Executive Bureau-Legislative Committee Relations,* Studies in Political Science No. 13, Random House, New York, 1955.

departments and the White House, all are restrained somewhat by the anti-executive lobbying law, but as explained by one of them: "We violate it [the spirit of the law] almost every day."

In the legislative system, the principal actors recognize the right of private and public groups as well as the executive to strive for their own points of view. Indeed, legislators seek out and cooperate with lobbyists from these groups. Under such circumstances, and given the primacy of the legislator in the lobbyist-legislator relationship, the system has its own built-in controls over lobbying which are more realistic and more effective than are the legalities of the lobby law regulations. It is plausible to argue that improvements in the operation, organization, and morality of the legislatures are far more important long-range factors than anything else in ensuring that effective controls and restrictions operate against improper lobbying by special interest groups.

CHAPTER 5

Lobbying the Executive and the Judiciary

INTEREST GROUPS are frequently as deeply involved in lobbying with the executive as they are with the legislature. Public policy is made also by members of the executive, and the public administration is entrusted to them. It is to be expected, therefore, that interest groups will seek to shape or affect executive decisions and administration. The narrow legal definition of lobbying in the Federal Regulation of Lobbying Law of 1946 that confines it to direct efforts at influencing the decisions of legislators simply ignores the realities of politics. Lobbying in the legislature is often part of an effort to affect the executive, just as intervention by interest groups in the executive may represent an effort to influence legislative policy.

As with interest groups and legislators, a useful framework for examining interest group-executive relations is that of mutual dependency and cooperation. Both sets of actors—the heads of the executive agencies and those representing the interest groups—need the other to accomplish their respective goals. They are dependent upon each other for services, information, support, and cooperation without which each would be disadvantaged in his own way.

Sanctions may be imposed upon the executive by the interest groups and vice versa. On the whole, sanctions invoked by interest groups against executives are probably more effective than against legislators. In contrast with their counterparts in Great Britain, the ruling American political party and the governmental executive are generally not integrated, unified systems of power. Administrative agencies are vulnerable not only to executive leaders and to political parties but also—and this constitutes a critical difference—to the legislature. And legislators at the national level are much less vulnerable to their parties, to political executives, and to administrative agencies.

Executives View Interest Groups As Useful Adjuncts

Both the political executive and the administrative agency head exist in a highly political environment. The nature of their programs, personnel, organization, and financial support as well as the effectiveness of their services or regulations may be sharply affected by others.

Those actors who may influence their operations are located in the legislature, the political parties, the interest groups, the rest of the executive establishment, and in other governmental units of the federal system.

Executive leaders require assistance; over the long run they cannot by themselves function successfully or survive as they wish. Decisions affecting them are not made solely or primarily on the bases of the merit of their programs and the effectiveness of their services or regulations. Executives and agencies are often confronted, moreover, by interest groups, legislators, other executive heads, and agencies who are hostile or who place a higher premium on other agencies and functions. That outside interest groups can help executives maintain counter pressures against forces intruding upon them was pointed out by one career official at the Brookings Institution's Round Table on federal executives in 1957–58: "The smart executive must be active in organizations outside of government in order to mobilize their support when he needs it. If he can organize counter pressure, he can maintain the integrity of his program despite the pressures seeking to influence his behavior."[1]

In this respect, most executive agencies have built-in allies. Those interest groups whose members are being serviced or regulated by an agency develop special relations with it. For example, the AFL-CIO acts as a clientele group for the U.S. Department of Labor, the agricultural interest groups for the Department of Agriculture, and business groups for the Department of Commerce. Indeed, the three departments were created in part because these groups campaigned for their establishment. In addition, different subsystems in the executive may have their own partisans, such as the education interest groups who maintain special relations with the U.S. Office of Education in the Department of Health, Education, and Welfare. From the point of view of the executive actor, these groups represent the clientele of his agency. The legislator sees his constituents as his principal clientele; the administrator finds his along functional rather than geographical lines. Not all executive agencies are endowed with the type of clientele groups that can act as useful adjuncts. Spokesman for the State Department and the foreign aid agency assume that they are relatively weak and defenseless in the Congress because they have no strong, natural clientele groups. It is their lament that only "do-gooder" civic or intellectual groups, who are relatively ineffectual in mobilizing public opinion and operating confidently in

[1] Quoted in Marver H. Bernstein, *The Job of the Federal Executive,* The Brookings Institution, Washington, D.C., 1958, p. 133.

the Congress, devote themselves to supporting the State Department and foreign aid policies.[2]

A second set of interest groups available to the executive actor for the support or defense of his agency are the professional groups from whose ranks most of the professional administrative staff is chosen. Unions and professional groups of policemen and firemen are concerned with police and fire departments; similarly, social welfare groups often act as allies of commissioners of welfare. And on the fringes, because their concern encompasses a variety of issues and functions other than those concentrated in any one agency, is a third type, the more general interest groups that may be sympathetic: the League of Women Voters, the General Federation of Women's Clubs, religious, economic, and civic groups.

There is a fourth type of interest group whose establishment is stimulated, if not initiated, by the principal executive actors. When these executives perceive an agency or program to be in difficulty and in need of maximum support, but that possesses no natural constituency or clientele of its own, they may help fashion one. The foreign aid program, which has increasingly encountered congressional resistance, was supported in 1964 by such a group that the President, as chief executive, helped create. The Committee for a National Trade Policy was also organized, at the initiation of the chief executive, to provide a strong spokesman for liberal foreign trade legislation. When the Administration discovered that it was in trouble on its general tax bill in the Ways and Means Committee in 1963, a Business Committee for Tax Reduction was organized with White House and Treasury Department blessings to rally business support behind the Kennedy program for tax reduction and reform. Similarly, The Citizens' Committee for a National Service Corps, a bipartisan effort to establish a domestic peace corps, represented another group which the national executive helped initiate and in which Administration leaders played a role.

Executive leaders can employ a variety of techniques for eliciting cooperation and support from interest groups. A number will be examined in the context of special situations, in order to illustrate techniques as well as to highlight the purposes for which executive actors utilize interest groups.

(A) COOPTING INTEREST GROUPS INTO GOVERNMENT The War Labor Board of World War II duration exemplifies efforts by leaders

[2] For an insight into the relative ineffectiveness of such groups see Bernard C. Cohen, *The Influence of Non-Governmental Groups on Foreign Policy Making,* World Peace Foundation, Boston, 1959, pp. 15–23.

of the executive to secure cooperation from interest groups by bringing them directly into the making of executive policy. No war effort could be successful if labor and business were to engage continuously in battles over wages, working conditions, and union recognition. To resolve conflict before it manifested itself on the production line and in strikes, representatives of business and labor were appointed to the War Labor Board along with spokesmen for the public interest. Management and labor often dissented from the decisions and opinions of the board. Nevertheless, to the extent that AFL and CIO leaders or management representatives participated in its decisions, they could not avoid being restrained and bound by the policies that the board helped formulate. As a coopting device, the board served as an extremely effective executive mechanism for fighting inflation and preventing labor strife from impairing the war effort.

(B) USING THE INTEREST GROUP TO PRESSURE THE POLITICAL EXECUTIVE   Attacks upon administrative agencies can originate from within the executive establishment. They are especially threatening when the political head of the executive decides to limit an agency. In order to thwart any reduction or abolishment of its functions, the agency must muster maximum support on the part of associated interest groups and direct it toward those influence points at which the political executive is most sensitive. The following case relates to a single subagency within a department, but it does illustrate a basic phenomenon of interest group-executive relations.

An executive decision to transfer the Children's Bureau from the Department of Labor to the Federal Security Agency, in 1946, raised serious prospects that the bureau would be reduced in function and possibly dissolved.[3] Discretion as to its future status was left in the hands of the administrator of the Federal Security Agency by the executive reorganization plan. When the head of the bureau learned of the extent of the administrator's power, outside friends and representatives of groups sympathetic to the bureau, such as the General Federation of Women's Clubs and labor groups, were alerted. They undertook to protest the transfer.

Since the chief of the bureau could obtain no assurance from the Federal Security Administrator that her unit would not be disbanded, she addressed herself to the President. In the meantime, her friendly interest groups had bombarded his office with letters requesting that the bureau be kept intact. While the President refused to commit

[3] "The Transfer of the Children's Bureau," in Harold Stein, ed., *Public Administration and Policy Development, A Case Book,* Harcourt, Brace & Co., New York, 1952, pp. 15–29.

himself on instructing the administrator to preserve the status of the bureau, he agreed to her suggestion for a letter of assurance which would molify the women's groups agitating for the bureau. The President's letter reiterated his refusal to interfere with the administrator, but it also indicated that any proposed basic change by the administrator affecting the bureau was to be discussed with the President before it went into effect. Moreover, the letter contained a statement that the President was confident the bureau's interests would be protected and even strengthened. Once the friends of the Children's Bureau were notified of the President's assurances, they immediately discontinued their campaign.

(C) CONSULTATION—FORMAL AND INFORMAL—FOR INFORMATION, ADVICE, AND UNDERSTANDING   An executive unit that services or regulates part of the general public needs the cooperation of those who are the recipients of its activities. As active organized units representing such recipients, interest groups have much to offer to an administrative or political executive. They can provide an alternative pipeline of information and ideas to that of the administrative bureaucracy. They may furnish special staff services for which the agency has neither the appropriations nor the skills, or that it considers too sensitive politically to undertake. They can feed back to the administrator the feelings and discontent of those most affected by his agency. Within his administrative frame of reference, therefore, they are valuable adjuncts of his leadership and useful allies for his agency.

This assistance is accomplished through informal as well as formal consultation with interest groups. On the local governmental level, the Director of the Budget for New York City has often utilized an interest group, the Citizens' Union, to prepare fiscal reports for his office. And the Citizens' Budget Commission, another such group, has carried out management surveys on a number of city departments for the mayor. An agency head is wise to keep in contact socially and professionally and on the job with the thinking of group leaders. But institutional means have also been devised, initiated often by the executive head, to assure the conduct of this relationship on a more systematic basis. Advisory boards and commissions are one of the principal formal techniques employed by the executive for tying in with and utilizing interest groups. When, for example, the Division of Grazing was first established in the Interior Department, it realized that it needed the cooperation of the western cattlemen who were to be restrained from overusing the land. To accomplish this objective, the division established an Advisory Board of ranchers who were elected by the cattlemen holding permits to graze.

Some regulatory commissions, both on the national and the state levels, are not staffed for the detailed, costly research that must precede administrative decisions on proposals emanating from outside its ranks. The Federal Communications Commission often submits proposals on rules initiated from within the television industry to an all-industry advisory committee in the hope that the research and development staffs of competing firms will provide the FCC with countervailing influences by which the public interest may be served. But, one such result, it has been contended, is "that the FCC becomes a captive of the television industry . . . that the FCC is charged with regulating."[4] It is characteristic of the close relationship between special regulatory agencies and those whom they regulate that the former tend to become especially sympathetic to the problems and aspirations of the latter; indeed, the agencies often act as their advocates.

A study of the problems of a newly created agency within a state, the Central and Southern Florida Flood Control District, reveals the multiplicity of purposes to which groups can be used at times.[5] The chief executive officer of the Flood Control District's governing board sponsored the formation of county water conservation and flood control committees. Representatives of every interest group concerned with water control—cattle, farm, industry, real estate, chambers of commerce, wildlife groups, and other governmental agencies—served on these county committees. The committees were organized to encourage grass roots support for the agency and for a water control plan that the executive proposed. They served as channels through which local wishes regarding drainage and reclamation portions of the project were communicated to the district.

Sometimes the executive has to devote himself diligently to the task of establishing the proper rapport with his clientele groups so that both can work together in an atmosphere of mutual trust. In 1963, a new U.S. Commissioner of Education undertook to work carefully with all the interest groups concerned with education in an effort to draw them into close, cooperative relations with his office and the Department of HEW. He made a special effort to bring them into the thinking of the department on education legislation and to give them the feeling that the constituency actually meant something to the new secretary of HEW as well as to himself. The cooperative, trusting relationship which this approach created helped produce

[4] William W. Boyer, *Bureaucracy on Trial,* The Bobbs-Merrill Co., Inc., Indianapolis, 1964, pp. 59–60.

[5] John De Grove, *The Florida Flood Control District,* Inter-University Case Program, No. 58, New York, 1960.

unity behind federal aid to education within a badly divided constituency. His efforts and results may be contrasted with the resentful reaction of such groups toward a former Secretary of HEW who, at his first formal meeting with the group representatives of this constituency, virtually told them that they were useless and unnecessary to the department. Many of these groups, traditionally allied with HEW on education, came to feel isolated from the department on this issue and excluded from its legislative strategy. Consequently, their lobbyists and officers became distrustful and antagonistic toward the political head of the department and his approach to education legislation.

(D) BUILDING POLITICAL STRENGTH IN THE LEGISLATURE   It is in the legislature that administrative agencies are often most vulnerable and in an environment generally less congenial than in the executive. Because their authorizations and appropriations must receive legislative sanction, agencies are particularly sensitive to legislative attitudes of approval or disapproval. A hostile or indifferent legislature may cut the agency's appropriations, alter or even eliminate programs, dictate administrative policy and procedures, and harass its personnel. Within the legislature, moreover, parts of the executive may find support for challenging other agencies and for resisting the political leadership in the executive.

Leaders at various levels of the executive seek to rally the support of their clientele groups as well as other more general groups that are friendly to them. A classic example of the success of an agency in building political support in the legislature in its conflicts with competing agencies and even in warding off the President, himself, is the U.S. Corps of Engineers.[6] Although only a subordinate unit of the Department of the Army and the Defense Department, the Corps has consistently sought to establish the position that, with regard to civil projects, it was responsible to Congress. On flood control policy and projects, it has operated as an independent unit, making its own arrangements with the Congress, and on terms satisfactory to itself.

In its disputes with Interior's Bureau of Reclamation over which should conduct public works projects, and in resisting Presidents, who have sought to control its activities, the Corps has been greatly assisted by the influence of its major clientele groups. The support of

---

[6] Stephen K. Bailey and Howard D. Samuel, *Congress at Work,* Henry Holt and Co., New York, 1952, Chapter 7, "Pork: Rivers and Harbors and Flood Control Act, 1950"; "The Kings River Project," in Stein, *op. cit.,* pp. 533–72; Robert De Roos and Arthur A. Maass, "The Lobby That Can't Be Licked," *Harper's Magazine,* Vol. 199, No. 1191, August 1949, pp. 21–30.

local interest groups has been actively cultivated by the Corps wherever it has operated; and it has played an important role within the principal, national interest group into which these locally powerful groups are organized, the Rivers and Harbors Congress. The Rivers and Harbors Congress has consisted not only of representatives from groups that benefit from flood control projects throughout the country or are associated with flood control problems but also representatives of the Corps of Engineers, itself, and of the U.S. Congress. Corps officials who work in civil projects automatically become members of the Rivers and Harbors Congress.

Of greatest importance to this interest group and its ally, the Corps, has been the participation in the Rivers and Harbors Congress of a bipartisan bloc from the national legislature, often the chairmen and sub-committee chairmen with their ranking minority party counterparts on the committees concerned with public works authorizations and appropriations. These legislators have sat in on the hearings of the Rivers and Harbors Congress at which time local groups have presented their project proposals for support by the Rivers and Harbors Congress in the national legislature. When, therefore, the Corps has waged its battles against the Bureau of Reclamation and the President, it has found a strong ally in an interest group that included the senior bipartisan bloc of congressmen who were required to judge and act upon the Corps' claims for jurisdiction, authorization, and appropriations. And lobbying with individual legislators have been the local interest groups who make up the Rivers and Harbors Congress.

Where an agency without such legislative support is caught in a conflict between major interest groups associated with the department of which it is a subunit, it can be severely penalized in the legislature. The Farm Security Administration was concerned primarily with alleviating the plight of low income rural people. Unfortunately, it was viewed with suspicion by the most powerful, general farm group, the American Farm Bureau Federation, and with hostility by key legislators on the appropriations committees of the Congress. In the face of this alliance, its political support from the Secretary of Agriculture, the Farmers' Union, the National Grange, and friendly urban forces proved inadequate to rescue the FSA. Its appropriations were drastically restricted in 1943, part of its functions was transferred to another agricultural agency, and eventually it was totally eliminated.

(E) ASSISTING THE POLITICAL EXECUTIVE LEADERSHIP IN THE LEGISLATURE   Traditionally, the national executive has not been a unified, integrated system responding to leadership from the top. The bureaus within the departments have been able to establish their own lines of access and influence with the Congress, while the department heads have been handicapped in developing any comparable political relations. The narrow, segmental interests of the bureaus have more easily been integrated into the legislative system and bolstered by their coalitions of interest groups.[7] Secretaries of departments have found themselves without the general support from interest groups to campaign effectively for a departmental position in the Congress.

Since 1949, when the first Hoover Commission called for the strengthening of the political heads of the departments, the departmental secretaries have begun to create the special staff for attracting to themselves and for their campaigns in the Congress the support of the major interest groups. Through the institutionalization of "executive lobbyists" at the departmental level, interest groups have been brought increasingly into partnership with the political executive so as to upgrade his efforts in the Congress. Each of the departments now contains a key assistant to the secretary who is responsible for advising him on congressional relations. This assistant acts as a legislative liaison or congressional relations officer. In the State Department, the importance of the function is attested to by its being assigned to an Assistant Secretary of State for Congressional Affairs; while in HEW, the Assistant Secretary for Legislation recently assumed full responsibility for substantive legislative liaison with Congress as well as for legislative programming, that is, the development of legislative proposals within the department. Only in the State Department is the task of working with the major interest groups the principal responsibility not of the special "executive lobbyist" but of the Assistant Secretary for Public Affairs whose position, it has been pointed out, was established to help organize the constituency of State behind its programs in the Congress.

As "executive lobbyist" for the secretary, the departmental legislative liaison agent serves as a key link between the secretary and the interest groups and as one of their major channels to the political executive. The liaison officers frequently help put together the intergroup coalitions behind departmental bills. They work in and with

---

[7] The more influential role of the bureaus over that of the departments in the Congress has been explored by J. Leiper Freeman, *The Political Process: Executive Bureau-Legislative Committee Relations,* Studies in Political Science 13, Random House, New York, 1955; The Commission on Organization of the Executive Branch of the Government, *Task Force Report on Departmental Management,* GPO, Washington, D.C., 1949, Parts I and II.

these coalitions, sharing information and planning strategy and tactics together. And the liaison agents endeavor to coordinate into the department's position the special clientele group relations that exist with the bureaus.

As a result, the political executive in the administration in Washington has become a key focal point around which interest groups revolve. This has enabled the political leaders to exert greater control over the legislative relations of their departments with the Congress and with outside groups. Consequently, departmental legislation has increasingly mustered the mass interest group support which the Hoover Commission's task force found so glaringly deficient in 1949.

Similar staff has emerged in the White House. A special congressional relations staff has been established close to the President that works actively with interest groups in mobilizing their support behind White House programs in the legislature. In addition, the President's substantive issue aides have their own pipelines to outside interest groups. At times, the two staffs are supplemented by a special organization established to campaign for a major piece of legislation that also negotiates with interest groups. Such was the case in 1962 when the Kennedy White House created a special unit to head up and integrate the campaign behind the Administration's proposed Trade Expansion Act.

It is not merely the national executives who rally interest groups behind their efforts to pass, stop, or alter legislation. In a number of states, the governor appoints a legislative counsel to act as his liaison agent with the state legislature and to deal with interest groups. An assistant to the mayor of New York City serves as his representative in Albany with the legislature. Among his responsibilities is the enlisting of support from interest groups and other allies of the city for the city's legislative program.

Interest Groups Interact With Executives

To the extent that political leaders or administrators need or want the services, cooperation, advice, and political support of interest groups, the latter are afforded legitimate roles by which to advance their own claims upon the executive. The strategy of executives in incorporating interest groups into their total posture of strength coincides with the needs of interest groups to have a voice in executive affairs.

Interest groups may desire a variety of responses from the executive. They range from a delegation of authority and power to make authoritative executive decisions, control over the appointment of key personnel, and a voice in the making and implementing of policy to some say in the staffing of the agency, consultation by and access to the head and staff of the administrative unit, and favorable attitudes and actions on the part of executive actors. In essence, clientele and other interest groups desire an "inside" position in the administrative agency, preferably at the top, with access to and influence upon those who conceive and develop policy and who make the rules by which it is administered.

Interest groups may also resort to a number of sanctions in order to achieve objectives which political executives and administrative officials cannot afford to ignore. Executive officialdom cannot afford to overlook the fact that interest groups may relate intimately with one or all of 'the following which can directly affect them: The legislature from which the agency receives its money and authority; the political executive actor who proposes its budget and who has his own set of political priorities; the specific publics who are regulated or serviced by the agency and whose cooperation is needed; the general public whose hostility may make administrators particularly vulnerable. Not all interest groups can successfully invoke sanctions, but executive actors must consider the claims advanced by such groups in the context of their potential for enforcing such claims.

(A) INFLUENCING THE APPOINTMENT OF EXECUTIVE PERSONNEL Having a voice in the selection of the top executive personnel of an agency can provide an interest group with a vital "in" on policy procedures. It can represent an important advantage for favorable access and for determining issues in a manner agreeable to the interest group and its members. If the group is not permitted to select the administrative or political official, it may try to exercise a veto over the appointment, determine what names will be considered, or at least propose the qualifications that nominees must meet. Although some groups are powerful enough politically or sufficiently close to an agency to affect personnel selections, few have any influence outside the one or two agencies with which they are vitally concerned. In an effort to retain its voice in the selection of agency personnel, an interest group will do battle, often going outside the executive system to bring pressure upon it from others more powerful politically.

Interest groups that are politically close to the leadership of a party which controls the executive branch of government have tremendous advantages. In agencies of particular concern to these groups, they receive special benefits: In placing their own representatives in the executive they affect policy and administration. The AFL-CIO was not only able to place one of its key leaders as Secretary of Labor in the Kennedy Administration but also the under secretary when a new secretary assumed office; moreover, one of the new assistant secretaries in the department had been a prominent union lobbyist. Another union official was made a key administrator in the Housing and Home Finance Agency, which was also close to labor's interests. Under the Eisenhower Administration, representatives of the American Farm Bureau Federation and its allies were given certain pivotal posts in the Agriculture Department. When the Kennedy Administration assumed power, some spokesmen for the Farmers' Union, a close ally of the Democratic leadership, were placed in decision-making positions.

When groups that endeavor to determine personnel selection are remote from an agency and not particularly powerful in the legislature or in the rest of the executive, their chances for success are slim. In the politics surrounding the disposal of surplus government property after World War II, various groups sought to influence the selection of those who would make the key policy decisions.[8] Both the Spokane and Portland Chambers of Commerce tried to block the employment as a consultant to the Surplus Property Board of a representative from the Bonneville Power Administration who was opposed to the disposal of aluminum plants to the Aluminum Company of America. With the information an Alcoa representative provided him, a senator raised the issue of the applicant's suitability on the floor of the Congress. This effort to interfere with the selection of an important staff adviser on surplus disposal failed. The Oregon interest groups involved were too unimportant to the agency, and they could not put together enough political "muscle."

A clientele group may feel that it has a vested right to be consulted in the selection and retention of key personnel. If the group has wider political affiliations or great respect in the political community, its position can sometimes prevail over the executive. If it does not, the administrator still runs the risk of transforming a powerful friend into an equally powerful enemy.

Three cases relating to interest group conflict with administrators illustrate different facets of this relationship. The district advisory boards of western stockmen, which had been established by the Interior Department's Grazing Service in order to secure the cooperation of these cattlemen, subsequently organized state advisory

[8] "The Disposal of the Aluminum Plants," in Stein, *op. cit.*, pp. 323–24.

boards and a National Advisory Board Council.[9] The original director of the Grazing Service had deferred to the National Council's advice against imposing higher fees on cattlemen whose livestock was permitted to graze on public land. Apparently the National Council came to expect that the Grazing Service and the Secretary of Interior would heed its advice. Therefore, when the secretary appointed a new director with a high fee orientation and not the candidate whom the council had recommended, it reacted adversely. The National Council felt that its advice had been disregarded and, even worse, that the secretary had never intended to act in accordance with its suggestion. Once the new agency head began to press for higher fees, the National Council unanimously opposed him. The powerful chairman of a subcommittee of the Senate Committee on Public Lands, Pat McCarran (Nev. D), a strong advocate of the stockmen of his state, also joined the attack. Consequently, the secretary, who initially sustained his director, had to recede from his position.

When the Grazing Service was further threatened by a hostile House Appropriations subcommittee that was angered because the agency had resisted imposing adequate fees, Senator McCarran once more attacked the agency, calling for a change in its administration. Stockmen's associations and the advisory boards created an *ad hoc* lobby, The Joint Livestock Committee on Public Lands, to defeat the proposed fee increases. This lobbying unit also approved the severe cuts in appropriations for the Grazing Service which the House committee had proposed. Caught between a Senate committee articulating the stockmen's demands for lower rates and a House committee insisting upon higher fees, the director of the Grazing Service was also confronted by an antagonistic interest group that normally would have been an ally but that now supported both committees in their attack upon his agency. Subsequently, the Grazing Service's budget was cut approximately 50 per cent, and its director was relieved of his duties.

In late 1964, the secretary of the U.S. Department of Labor demanded the resignation of his chief subordinate, the under secretary. He was immediately challenged by the president of the AFL-CIO. Apparently no policy differences existed between the secretary and his subordinate; rather, the secretary wanted someone in the second position of leadership with whom he had better personal and intellectual rapport. However, the AFL-CIO regarded the occupant of the under secretary's post as labor's chief spokesman in the govern-

---

[9] Phillip O. Foss, *The Grazing Fee Dilemma,* The Inter-University Case Program, No. 57, New York, 1960.

ment. Since the labor leadership was so closely associated politically with the Democratic Administration and the AFL-CIO constituted the department's chief clientele group, it was crucial to all concerned that the conflict be resolved amicably. Reportedly, U.S. Supreme Court Justice Arthur J. Goldberg, who had served previously as Secretary of Labor, intervened to help settle the dispute. It is significant that the conflict was resolved by the secretary's decision to withdraw his demands for the under secretary's resignation. The leading clientele group had too much at stake and was too powerful politically to be thwarted on this key personnel decision.

Groups that are not massively engaged in partisan politics may also be influential because they are so highly respected that their active disapproval of an executive head may cause the latter to become politically vulnerable. In alienating the scientific community, the political leader of an executive department found himself suspect by those whose cooperation he required in running his subordinate agencies.[10] Moreover, he also discovered that the general public could be aroused against thim and that the opposition party in the legislature was alert to capitalize politically upon his errors.

Secretary of Commerce Sinclair Weeks had come to his department, as had so many in the new Eisenhower team, suspicious of Washington bureaucrats and alert for demonstrable proof that they were harassing businessmen. A small firm, which had been engaged in a running battle with the Federal Trade Commission and the Post Office Department, was faced with a negative scientific analysis of its product, a battery additive, by the Commerce Department's Bureau of Standards. An appeal from the president of the firm apparently confirmed the secretary's suspicions regarding a bureaucratic lack of sympathy with legitimate business practices. Weeks summarily asked for the resignation of the bureau's director, a nationally prominent scientist.

A number of professional and clientele groups associated with the Bureau of Standards campaigned to coerce the secretary to reinstate the scientific head of the chief United States testing agency. In their eyes, he had been removed for political reasons alone, and scientific judgment was being prostituted for partisan purposes. The furor which these groups and their allies in the general community stimulated reached such magnitude that the secretary was compelled to retreat. When the Advisory Committee to the bureau, on which were represented some of the top scientists of the National Academy of

[10] Samuel A. Lawrence, *The Battery Additive Controversy,* The Inter-University Case Program, No. 68, New York, 1962.

Sciences, instructed him to reinstate the director, the secretary found himself challenged by the leaders in the most respected scientific body in the country. No Secretary of Commerce could effectively operate the Bureau of Standards without the cooperation and good will of the scientific community. Moreover, the Democrats seized upon the issue and exploited it as a major political scandal. In the end, the director was reinstated, tests were conducted again on the battery additive, and the scientific judgment of the director and his colleagues was fully confirmed.

(B) FAVORED TREATMENT BY THE EXECUTIVE For many years, until the middle of the Eisenhower Administration, a very close relationship existed at the national, state, and local levels between the American Farm Bureau Federation and the Extension Service in the Department of Agriculture.[11] The service benefited greatly from this support by the largest and most powerful of the general farm interest groups. Its lowest operating unit, the county agent, was supported financially and organizationally by the county Farm Bureaus. Through either mandatory or permissive state legislative statutes, the local Farm Bureaus were designated the sponsoring units which permitted extension funds to be spent in a county. Consequently, many county agents, paid in part and dependent upon the interest group, allied themselves with the Farm Bureau; they solicited and recruited members for it. Dues for the state Farm Bureau and the national federation were collected in semigovernmental units which served at the same time as basic units for the favored interest group. There is little doubt, moreover, that many county agents treated Farm Bureau members in their counties much more favorably than farmers who belonged to comparable agricultural groups. On the basis of its association with the Extension Service, the Farm Bureau had, in fact, emerged as the largest of all the agricultural interest groups.

At the national level, the National Farm Bureau Federation worked hand in hand with key legislators and/or the Secretary of Agriculture to expand the function of the Extension Service. It also sought to increase its appropriations in the executive budget at the expense of the action agencies, such as the Soil Conservation Service, which had their own clientele groups and which the NFBF considered a threat to its influence upon agricultural policy. Ultimately, pressure from a number of organized groups—the Farmers' Union, the National Grange, private insurance companies—and congressmen more sympathetic to other agricultural agencies forced a separation between

11 William J. Block, *The Separation of the Farm Bureau and the Extension Service, Political Issue in a Federal System,* The University of Illinois Press, Urbana, 1960, pp. 211–15.

the two. Secretary of Agriculture Ezra T. Benson, the director of the Extension Service, and the Farm Bureau, itself, recognized that the agency had to be fully separated from the interest group if they were to allay congressional suspicions regarding an expanding Extension Service.

(C) INFLUENCING POLICY   Clientele groups often pursue their own short-range goals which may cause them to clash with executive agencies that are sympathetic and clientele oriented. During World War II, the AFL-CIO launched an aggressive campaign against the scientific objectivity and reliability of the cost of living index compiled by the Bureau of Labor Statistics, an agency originally created through the efforts of union labor.[12] This attack by a clientele group on a key statistical tool of its agency seriously threatened to undermine general public confidence in the index. Government, business, labor, and the public were accustomed to relying upon the index in planning and in making vitally important decisions.

The drive against the cost of living index was actually part of a massive effort by organized labor to breach the government's wage formula. Union research directors and top union leaders criticized the index in private consultation with the bureau and the Secretary of Labor as well as the President, and they forced the issue into the public arena. Business groups rallied to the defense of the index, but the attack had become so political and public that the President appointed a special committee to resolve the conflict; both major labor federations and the Administration were represented on it. This committee successfully deflated the campaign against the index.

If clientele groups are divided or uninterested in controversial policy proposals initiated by their agency, the latter may become vulnerable to attack by other groups which strongly oppose this policy. An administrative decision by a semi-independent federal agency, the United States Bureau of the Census, was overruled by the highest political quarters when nonclientele groups mounted an attack upon a census question on religion.[13]

The Census of Religious Bodies had been discontinued in 1946 for a number of reasons, including Christian Science opposition. After careful preparatory work, the Director of the Bureau of the Census proposed, in 1956, to insert a religious question in the 1960 census. His decision reflected the desires of professional groups of social scientists and certain religious groups, particularly the Roman Catholic Church that had approved such a question at the National Catholic

---

[12] "The Attack on the Cost of Living Index," in Stein, *op. cit.,* pp. 775–853.
[13] Charles R. Foster, *A Question on Religion,* The Inter-University Case Program, No. 66, New York, 1961.

Welfare Conference in 1956. The Association of Statisticians of American Religious Bodies had indicated that it, too, favored such a question, leading the Director of the Census to believe that he had secured the approval of all the major denominations and religions. Moreover, a users advisory group had not reacted adversely when he announced his intentions.

Major opposition did materialize, however. The American Jewish Congress initiated a public campaign against including the question in the 1960 census. Its strong public position crystallized the opposing forces, and overnight the issue became a subject of public debate. Among the allies of the American Jewish Congress were the American Civil Liberties Union, some of the principal newspapers in the country, the Christian Scientists, Mormons, representatives of Protestant denominations, principally the Baptists, and the liberal Catholic weekly, *Commonweal*.

As a result of this debate, the director of the bureau decided against including the question. He was fearful that the controversy might lead to an unfavorable public reaction against the entire 1960 census. Furthermore, it was obvious that the business and governmental users of the census were not interested in the question, although the religious community was now divided. When the bureau did release data based upon a religious question in the March 1957 Current Population Survey, the opposition went all the way to the secretary of the department and to the White House. A Republican senator from Utah was even prevailed upon to appeal to the Assistant to the President, Sherman Adams. After consulting the White House, the Secretary of Commerce ordered the bureau not to publish any additional data or to include any further questions on the subject of religion. As a result, the second volume of the March Current Population Survey never appeared.

Students of public administration point out that interest groups are often responsible for the transferring of functions from one agency to another by the legislature. The group's membership may believe that it will be better served or less strictly regulated if another agency oversees it. When the meat packing industry decided that the Federal Trade Commission was regulating it too stringently, it prevailed upon the Congress to shift the regulatory responsibility to the Department of Agriculture.[14] Similarly, when conservationists concluded that the Department of the Interior was pursuing a "give away"

---

[14] Herbert A. Simon, Donald W. Smithburg, and Victor A. Thompson, *Public Administration*, Alfred A. Knopf, Inc., New York, 1962, pp. 170, 412–13.

philosophy, they succeeded in having transferred to the Department of Agriculture the activities of what is now the Forest Service.

Interest groups sympathetic to the Administration and able to exert some influence in the Congress can at times compel political executives to modify the legislation that they propose. To this writer's knowledge, at least two major allies of the Kennedy Administration applied pressure upon it to achieve such results. Labor felt threatened by a provision in the Administration's agricultural bill which permitted agricultural land to be developed into industrial parks. This was viewed by labor leaders as a possible opening wedge, especially in the South, that could be used by states to attract "run-away" shops, those fleeing from areas where union recognition and high wages prevailed. Labor lobbyists first contacted the under secretary of labor and ultimately the secretary, himself, in order to make evident that they would use their influence with their urban congressional friends to help kill the bill unless this provision were clarified to their satisfaction. This was accomplished. On at least two other occasions when the Administration was advancing major policy recommendations, the Trade Expansion Act of 1962 and the major tax bill of 1963, labor threatened to "change our position" on these bills unless, in one instance, provisions that it believed to be injurious to the interests of workers and unions were altered; and, in another, certain protective provisions were retained, provisions that Democratic legislative leaders thought had to be jettisoned in order to pass the bill in the House of Representatives.

The Farmers' Union, which was also close to the Kennedy Administration and its leadership in the Department of Agriculture, applied similar pressure upon the White House in defense of the department's and its own position. In 1962, its lobbyists threatened to look very critically at the trade bill unless the department's position in another, unrelated, area were liberalized. On two occasions, the Farmers' Union notified the White House that it would take a "hard" rather than a sympathetic look at the Kennedy tax bill, which at the time seemed to be in trouble in the Congress, unless the Administration requested greater appropriations for certain agricultural programs.

All of these bills were critical to the Administration, it should be stressed, and needed maximum support to pass in the form which it desired. Hence, there existed considerable opportunity for maneuver on the part of these interest groups. Their lobbyists and leaders worked with the heads of the departments and utilized the departmental legislative liaison staff as a communications link with the White House. If they are judged to be powerful or if they are close allies of the chief executive and his party, interest groups have access all the way from his legislative liaison staff through his substantive area assistants and his department heads to the President, himself.

On the state level, the governor is more accessible than is the President. He, too, may be utilized to intervene with his appointed department heads and to be of assistance in the legislature. In the 1965 North Carolina state legislature, for example, the competing private power companies and the rural electrification cooperatives worked out a compromise under the leadership of the governor, a compromise that the chief executive then sponsored in the legislature. The North Carolina League of Municipalities, which had not been invited to participate in these executive-interest group conferences and whose members felt injured by the terms of the compromise, found that it was unable, in the legislature, to overturn this combination or to force a modification in the compromise.

Conclusions

Interest groups want access to the elected and appointed executives and to career administrators of subordinate agencies. They want a sympathetic response to their proposals, a choice in or veto over some appointments, consultation—institutional and informal—to afford them a voice in the administrative policies and practices of the executive and in its legislative proposals. Members of the executive, on the other hand, need and want the cooperation, services, and political support that the interest groups can provide them within the executive system and within the legislature. Executive strategy and interest group strategy, therefore, often coincide.

The executive actor is much more vulnerable than is the legislator to interest group politics. Even groups that are not within "the constituency" of the executive agency can marshal sufficient pressure in and outside the executive system to affect executive decision-making. Adverse publicity in the press and in the constituency is feared by the administrator as well as the legislator. But the administrator is much more dependent upon the good will and cooperation of the legislators than are these decision-makers upon their constituencies—their electorates. Legislators need not return to their constituencies for reelection for two, four, or six years; and they can balance off one group against another, depending upon popular feeling to wane on many issues and relying upon party organization to support them.

The apprehension administrators share regarding bad publicity and attacks against them or their agencies arises, in good part, because they are dependent. They must rely on the good will of the legislature that is actually part of their constituency. Here their personnel, programs, procedures, and appropriations are amenable to change, and adversely inclined interest groups may be active and influential. Moreover, they may also become vulnerable within the executive system. At any time, they may be considered expendable under a different set of criteria by top political and appointed officers, and they must often compete with other executive agencies for funds and functions.

Despite these generalizations and the illustrations cited, it is erroneous to conclude that administrative and political executives respond like puppets to interest groups. As in the case of the legislators, they are not automatons who can always be pushed easily or even successfully in the direction preferred by the interest groups. Administrative as well as political executives may hold strong convictions of their own and possess inner, institutional, and political sources of strength. They frequently develop lines of communications and mutually satisfactory arrangements with key legislators and subsections of the legislative system. And they develop valuable relations with their political superiors. In addition, these executives conduct their own public relations programs to cultivate a favorable image with the general public. Within the executive system, career officials have the resiliency that comes from tenure, professional competence, formal power, and legislative support. Hence, agencies and departments can often withstand onslaughts by their own clientele groups. To the extent that his clientele and other groups are part of an executive actor's web of influence, the official is in an advantageous position to deal with attacks by outside interest groups and even legislators.

Comments by participants in the Brookings Institution's Round Table on the federal executive regarding the experiences of General Omar Bradley, one-time head of the Veterans Administration, demonstrate the strength of an independent, respected executive head and, at the same time, the power wielded by interest group clusters in this agency. Except for the general, all the Veterans Administration heads in the previous thirty years had been unwilling to take a public position different from that of the veterans' groups. The participants pictured General Bradley as an administrator "with outstanding courage" in standing up to the interest groups. Despite the hostility of most of the veterans' groups, he succeeded in persuading Congress to adopt recommendations that probably saved the taxpayers a billion dollars or more. However, he paid a price for his independence. He alienated the veterans' groups and was severely criticized for his independent stand. Moreover, he probably lost, thereby, their support for the recommendations that he subsequently made when serving as chairman of a commission studying veterans' benefits.

Does collaboration between the bureaucracy and the interest group unnecessarily maximize the particular interests of the group and the agency at the expense of the public interest? No absolute answer can be offered. In all probability it does sometimes, just as it frequently works for the public interest.

On the whole, it is the glaring example of malfeasance in executive-interest group relationships or the adverse effects upon the public interest that elicit headlines and stimulate investigations. The day-to-day cooperative, useful relationships receive little publicity. Nevertheless, Marver H. Bernstein concluded from his conversations with Eisenhower Administration executives in the Brookings Institution's Round Table that, even though interest groups could assist administrators, such groups "were not conducive to the unity and rationality that executives strive to achieve."[15]

Other students of the relationship between public administration and interest groups emphasize more positive consequences. Aside from the political support that the executives build thereby for their programs, two other advantages will be mentioned here. Marshall E. Dimock and Gladys O. Dimock contend that interest groups provide a means for citizenship control over the bureaucracy. By injecting the concerned citizen's point of view into public administration, the interest group helps keep the bureaucracy alert and responsive. Moreover, they argue, interest groups act as a counterbalance to any "excess of professionalism." What emerges from the competition among them is "broader than the professional view of any one of them."[16]

This author's own research into the relationship between interest groups and the congressional relations officers of the executive departments in Washington leads him to conclude that interest groups, when they are tied into the legislative programming and politics of the heads of the departments, can also enable political executives to control more effectively their bureaucracies. To the extent that this is the case, a vital element in democratic theory is reinforced—that the politically responsible leaders of the executive control the making of public policy. Public policy, at least in terms of legislative programs and relations with the Congress, should be responsive to and under

[15] Bernstein, *op. cit.*, p. 136.
[16] Marshall E. Dimock and Gladys O. Dimock, *Public Administration*, 3rd edit., Holt, Rinehart, and Winston, Inc., New York, 1964, p. 389.

the control, as much as possible, of the politically elected and appointed executive officials, not the segmental parts of the bureaucracy, each of which may guard only its own particular set of interests.

Lobbying and the Judicial System[17]

Compared with legislators and members of the executive, judges, who constitute the principal actors in the judicial system, are insulated from outside political pressures. The ethics and "rules of the game" of the judicial process clearly stamp as improper or illegal much of the type of intervention characteristic of lobbying efforts in the legislature and the executive. Such tactics encounter immediate and often drastic sanctions on the part of the judges as well as the disapproval of legislators, executives, and the general public. The judicial process and judicial decisions are deemed to be of such a special nature as to preclude the intrusion of political forces from outside the courtroom.

Interest groups do intervene, however, in the judicial system, for the judiciary is merely another arena of government in which conflict may be resolved and authoritative decisions rendered on public policy. And a variety of levels of appeal exist in the judicial system. Those groups which fail or are disadvantaged in the executive, legislative, or party arenas often seek a more favorable decision by appealing to the judicial system. The judiciary has the power to overrule the legislature and the executive as well as to interpret the rules upon which either of the two decide. In the final resort, the judiciary can interpret the constitutions of the state and national governments.

Political considerations intrude, moreover, in the pre-judicial stages —in the nomination and selection of judges. Judges are chosen by joint action of the executive and the Senate in the national government and by executive appointment, election by the legislature, or by the general electorate at the state level. To the extent that interest groups wield influence in the party, the electorate, the legislature, or the executive, they can play a role in the nomination and selection of judges.

Lobbying to affect the selection of judicial actors or the determination of judicial policy is somewhat similar to that in the executive and

[17] I have relied heavily in this section on Walter F. Murphy and C. Herman Pritchett, eds., *Courts, Judges, and Politics, An Introduction to the Judicial Process*, Random House, New York, 1961, Chapter 8, "Interest Groups and Litigation"; Glendon A. Schubert, *Constitutional Politics, The Political Behavior of Supreme Court Justices and The Constitutional Policies That They Make*, Holt, Rinehart, and Winston, Inc., New York, 1960, pp. 46–51, 69–82; Glendon A. Schubert, *Judicial Behavior, A Reader in Theory and Research*, Rand, McNally & Co., Chicago, 1964, pp. 50–55, 191–92, 266, 270, 273–86.

legislative processes. On the whole, however, access is more difficult; and the whole area is much more circumscribed.

Influencing the Selection of Judges

In most instances, very few interest groups concern themselves with the judicial selection process. Nevertheless, judges are particularly significant decision-makers in the American political system, so that groups intervene, at times, either to veto those candidates whom they regard as holding views contrary or detrimental to their own or to ensure that candidates are chosen who are acceptable to them.

One professional interest group that concerns itself consistently with the nomination of judges—a group that carries considerable weight in the selection process—is the organized bar. In a number of states and in many of the larger cities, the bar association assumes responsibility for nominating suitable candidates. Often where political parties nominate judicial candidates who are chosen at the polls, as in New York, the local bar association evaluates these candidates. Not infrequently they report unfavorably on them. These ratings are publicized by the press, and thus the voter can readily obtain the evaluations of a nonpartisan professional group in determining whether to follow his political party's choices. Where the governors fill vacancies in the judiciary, or the legislators choose the judges, the endorsement of the bar association frequently provides a candidate with a decided advantage over others. On the national level, a negative report from a bar association's selection committee can injure a candidate's chances for confirmation in the Senate.

The most dramatic, and probably the only well-documented, example of an interest group's vetoing the selection of a judge occurred in the nomination of Federal Circuit Court Judge John J. Parker for the U.S. Supreme Court in 1930. A former North Carolina Republican leader, Judge Parker was nominated by President Herbert Hoover with respectable support from among members of the national and state judiciary, the U.S. Senate, and leaders of the outstanding legal interest groups, the national and state bar associations. He was bitterly opposed, however, by union labor and Negro groups. These groups had as allies a receptive group of liberal senators. The latter saw the issue as one of repudiating anti-labor and anti-Negro politics as well as administering a defeat to President Hoover. The charges against Parker stemmed from two separate incidents. During his campaign for governor, in 1920, he had warned that Negro participation in politics was a "source of evil and danger to both races" and "not desired by the Republican party of North Carolina"; as a federal judge, he had upheld an injunction to enforce a "yellow-dog" contract. When, at the urging of Negro and labor leaders, liberals in the Senate made a major issue of Parker's nomination, the Judiciary Committee reported unfavorably on his candidacy and he was rejected by a vote of 41 to 39.

In most cases, however, interest groups have not been able to rally sufficient strength to prevent a nomination to any national court. Organized labor unsuccessfully opposed President Taft's nomination to the U.S. Supreme Court of Mahlon Pitney, a former state Republican leader and a member of the New Jersey judiciary, who had ruled against peaceful picketing. Justice Louis A. Brandeis won nomination to the U.S. Supreme Court in spite of widespread opposition. And in the late 1950's and early 1960's, ultraconservative groups led by the John Birch Society made absolutely no progress in campaigning for the impeachment of Chief Justice Earl Warren of the U.S. Supreme Court.

The Strategy of "Amicus Curiae"

Interest groups may seek direct access via *amici* briefs to the courts when issues are important to them. Although they may not be a direct party to the case in conflict, they frequently are permitted to file briefs and/or present oral arguments before a court. In part, this constitutes a type of relationship characteristic of lobbyists with executives and legislators; both the judiciary and the interest groups have something to gain from each other. By providing the court with well-developed and often alternative legal approaches to the issue at conflict, the groups' interests coincide with the court's interest in arriving at a just decision. Courts have recognized that many cases raise issues that affect more than the contending parties. The courts, therefore, sometimes invite additional parties to submit briefs.

Thus the *amicus curiae* represents an opportunity for interest groups to intervene before a decision is made and to affect not only the immediate conflict but also the thinking of the court as it will affect future decisions. If the parties to the case and the court permit, concerned interest groups can mobilize their resources and prestige in order to elicit the type of authoritative decision that they desire. *Amici* briefs also afford interest groups an opportunity to join in temporary alliances with other groups to affect the decisions of the judges just as groups unite in common lobbying campaigns to influence legislators and executives.

At one time, the U.S. Supreme Court concluded that it was being unduly pressured by interest groups using the *amicus curiae* strategy. During the October 1948 term, seventy-five such briefs were filed in fifty-seven cases. In 1949, the Court limited this access to itself. The consent of all parties to the case at issue had to be obtained by any group desiring to file a brief as a "friend of the court." However, governmental units were still permitted to file such briefs although nongovernmental groups who were denied such access by the disputants in the case were permitted to request the Court's permission to intervene. This action radically diminished the opportunity for interest groups to participate in important cases of public policy.

For a time the United States Solicitor General refused to grant permission to any group to appear before the Supreme Court as *amicus curiae.* In approximately 50 per cent of the cases coming before the court the national government is a party; therefore, in about half of the court's cases, the judges were precluded from ready access to the briefs of interested parties. Complaints by some of the judges led the Solicitor General to modify his rigid policy. Not only have subsequent solicitors general adopted more liberal standards but also in cases where the government has refused consent, the Supreme Court has at times granted this permission.

Not all groups have equal access to the judiciary. The Court has granted access to certain interest groups but has denied it to others, depending upon their relation to the case. In the Steel Seizure case, the CIO was permitted to file a brief, whereas an American Legion post was refused permission. The latter group obviously had only a remote interest in the controversy.

At times, interest groups have brought the executive, itself, in as an *amicus curiae* in order to assist them in influencing the court. In *Shelley* v. *Baker,* the famous restrictive covenant case, the Solicitor General appeared as a friend of the Court, explaining that the Attorney General and he had been asked by organized groups to enter the case. Both students of the judicial process as well as interest groups recognize that *amici* briefs can be influential. Mr. Justice Frankfurter, for example, kept before him, during oral argument in the case of *Illinois ex. rel. McCollum* v. *Board of Education,* the brief of the American Jewish Congress that he used extensively in his concurring opinion.

Interest groups approach the judiciary in this manner at other levels of the federal system. In February, 1965, both the American Jewish Congress and the New York Civil Liberties Union had their motions to intervene as "friends of the court" denied by the New York Supreme Court judge presiding over a case that concerned the 1964 legislature's reapportionment plan.[18] He did grant this privilege to

---

[18] *New York Times,* February 6, 1965, p. 42.

a city mayor, a county executive, and to the radio station which had earlier initiated the challenge against the New York legislature.

The Use of Test Cases

Groups have utilized litigation in the courts to make public policy in the absence of legislative action. The basic strategy of the NAACP was conceived in terms of the courts, the one decision-making center where it enjoyed relatively equal access with all other groups. It has successfully employed the test case technique for bringing issues to the courts at the appropriate time and under the most propitious circumstances. The elements of timing and preparation are as critical in this strategy as they are in the legislative and executive systems. The NAACP deliberately selected and prepared those cases that would provide the best vehicle for a constitutional test. In pushing for improved rights and status for Negroes, the NAACP and its friends successfully induced the courts through litigation to make public policy in the absence of action by legislative bodies.

To accomplish this sustained and carefully conceived strategy, the NAACP had to develop the organizational apparatus, raise the necessary finances, and coordinate the efforts of Negro lawyers and allies throughout the country. In approaching the courts in this manner, organization was almost mandatory; the cost alone of each case won by the NAACP in the Supreme Court averaged $10,000. Obviously such a campaign can only be conducted through organized groups, which brings us back to an initial point in our study, the value of organization over individual action. This is particularly true in terms of the Negro who has tended to be socially and economically depressed and who has been especially susceptive to economic and legal coercion.

In organizing its approach to the judicial system, the NAACP afforded individual Negroes an opportunity to find effective representation before the judiciary. However, the NAACP found itself vulnerable to counter-attack in southern states. It was prosecuted on the grounds that it solicited lawsuits, that it stirred up legal quarrels, and that it paid individuals to bring suits. All these charges involved offenses under common law and often statute law. The federal courts have sustained the NAACP's arguments that the application of such statutes infringes upon the constitutional right of an interest group to solicit individuals to bring cases to court and to pay their expenses in order to achieve its policy aims. The courts have accepted the position that a group has a right to sue to protect the rights of its members.

Public Relations: Building Public Opinion to Which Judges Are Receptive

Just as they may seek to mobilize various publics in order that legislators and executives will respond to public opinion, interest groups may also seek to influence judges in this manner. Some groups have organized letter writing campaigns to the courts. The National Committee to Secure Justice in the Rosenberg case claimed, in 1953, that 50,000 persons supported its petition to the U.S. Supreme Court. On occasion, groups have resorted to the tactic of sending personal delegations in an attempt to affect judicial decisions. But none of these tactics is effective with the courts. Individual judges have expressed their strong disapproval of such efforts. After groups had picketed outside the court, in New York City, in protest against the trial of Communist leaders under the Smith Act, Congress made it a federal offense, in 1950, for persons to picket, parade, or demonstrate in or near a federal courthouse with intent to influence a judge or anyone else connected with a trial.

A more legitimate tactic exists by which interest groups can mold that public opinion which judges respect and to which they turn professionally for guidance. By resorting to the publication of articles in law journals, it is possible for such groups to influence the legal profession, and particularly the law schools and judges. Not only does the climate of opinion become more favorable to new legal theories and approaches in this manner but also judges rely upon the authority of such journals.

The NAACP's campaign against racial covenants in housing, for example, included an effort to influence legal opinion by utilizing law review articles in order to bring the outstanding sociological and economic critics of racial covenants to the attention of the judiciary and the legal profession. In addition, NAACP legal briefs cited these articles. Interest groups concerned with economic policy have also employed this approach. As a consequence of what seemed to him undue reliance by the U.S. Supreme Court upon such articles, Congressman Wright Patman (Texas D) has publicly attacked lobbying through law reviews and the practice of the Court in using such articles in its ruling against the government in anti-trust suits.[19] On the other hand, Chief Justice Earl Warren of the U.S. Supreme Court publicly expressed the opinion that the leading law review articles were making available to the judges some of the best legal thinking in the country.

[19] See *Congressional Record,* 85:1, Vol. 103, Part 12, August 27, 1957, pp. 16159–69.

CHAPTER 6

Interest Groups Bypass Lobbying to Legislate Directly[1]

OUR POLITICAL SYSTEM provides more favorable opportunities for interest groups to intervene in the decision-making processes and in the organization and operation of public administration than does any other system. Where else can such a variety of interest groups intercede so freely and profitably with the courts as well as in the legislature and the executive? Moreover, a fourth alternative exists in the United States to which interest groups in all but a very few of the other democratic political systems cannot address themselves. At the state and local levels of government and to a certain extent in one sector of national policy-making, interest groups may appeal directly to the electorate for authoritative decisions on issues that can bind the legislature, executive, and the courts.

[1] Data on interest group involvement in direct legislation campaigns is fragmentary. See Winston W. Crouch, *The Initiative and Referendum in California,* The Haynes Foundation, Los Angeles, 1950; Frank A. Pinner, Paul Jacobs, and Philip Selznick, *Old Age and Political Behavior, A Case Study,* University of California Press, Berkeley, 1959, Chapter VI, "Political Action," and pp. 270–71; Abraham Holtzman, *The Townsend Movement, A Political Study,* Bookman Associates, Inc., New York, 1963, pp. 193–98. See also two Eagleton Institute Case Studies in Practical Politics, Robert S. Walker and Samuel C. Patterson, *Oklahoma Goes Wet: The Repeal of Prohibition,* McGraw-Hill Book Co., Inc., New York, 1960; and Gordon E. Baker, *The Politics of Reapportionment in Washington State,* McGraw-Hill Book Co., Inc., New York, 1960. A number of recent articles deal with various campaigns by interest groups: Gordon E. Baker, "Reapportionment by Initiative in Oregon," *Western Political Quarterly,* Vol. XIII, No. 2, June 1960, pp. 508–19; John S. Radabaught, "Tendencies of California Direct Legislation," *Southwestern Social Science Quarterly,* Vol. 42, No. 1, June 1961, pp. 66–77; James A. Maxwell, "Ohio: The Battle Bricker Didn't Want," *The Reporter,* Vol. 19, No. 9, Nov. 27, 1958, p. 19; Steven Warshaw, "California: The Union Shop and the Amendment Game," *The Reporter,* Vol. 19, No. 7, October 30, 1958, pp. 14–16; Thomas S. Barclay, "The Reapportionment Struggle in California in 1948," *Western Political Quarterly,* Vol. 41, No. 2, June 1959, pp. 313–24; Richard L. Neuberger, "Government by the People," *Survey,* Vol. LXXXVI, No. 11, November 1950, pp. 490–93; Abraham Holtzman, "Fluoridation: Lessons in Civic Reform," *The Bulletin of the American Association of Public Health Dentists,* Vol. 18, No. 2, June 1958, pp. 2–6.

Direct Legislative Politics at the State and Local Levels of Government

The extent of direct legislative and constitutional power in the hands of the electorate—through the initiative and the referendum—virtually makes the American system *sui generis*. In all the states, constitutional amendments proposed by the state legislatures must be ratified by a vote of the people. Many states must submit other public decisions, such as bond issues, to the electorate. In addition, twenty states and a great many units of local government permit groups in the electorate to initiate statutory and/or constitutional proposals upon which the general electorate and not the legislature acts. And laws adopted by legislative bodies can be referred by the proper action of interest groups to the ballot for reconsideration by the people.

The Initiative and Referendum

An initiative is a constitutional device whereby a small percentage of the electorate may on its own action, by securing a requisite number of signatures through the public circulation of petitions, place upon the ballot a policy issue for a public vote. There are at least three major types of initiatives. Two bypass the legislature completely: one places a statutory law on the ballot for a vote; the other, a constitutional amendment. The third, an "indirect" initiative, affords the legislature an opportunity to act upon a proposal after it has been presented to the legislature via the petition-signature route. The legislators may enact the measure or propose an alternative of their own. Should they change the proposal or refuse to adopt it as proposed, it must go on the ballot with or without a legislative alternative. An interesting variation is the "advisory" initiative which also bypasses the legislature and places a policy proposal on the ballot for a non-binding vote by the electorate.

Three types of referenda are most commonly used. The "compulsory" referendum does not require a petition by the citizenry. Under constitutional mandate, certain legislative measures—bond issues and constitutional amendments—must be placed upon the ballot for final decision by the voters. Another type involves the collection of sufficient signatures on a special petition from among the electorate in order to suspend the operation of an act passed by the legislature and to refer the act to the ballot for a popular vote. The third type is the "advisory" referendum that has been employed by many city councils and by at least two states. However, the legislative body retains full power to act because the public vote is advisory in nature only.

During the period 1962–63, the electorate in more than four fifths of the states voted directly on legislation. In the great majority of such cases, voters acted upon referenda submitted by the legislature. But a number of policy issues were placed upon the ballot by petition initiatives and referenda.

Almost every kind of interest group has used the initiative as a strategic approach to policy-making: labor, farmer, education, religious, civic, gambling, old age, ideological, and business. Over the long run, business groups have resorted more to the referendum than to the initiative. One explanation is that business groups generally do not desire major legislation of a positive nature; rather the referendum affords these groups a tool by which they can attempt to alter or repeal legislative or initiative action aimed at them or that they feel is detrimental to their interests. That business groups make active use of the initiative, however, is exemplified by "right-to-work" laws prohibiting the "union shop," which they have placed on the ballot in a number of states, some of which have been adopted.

The Advantages of Direct Legislation Over Lobbying

Lobbying in the legislature, the courts, or the executive is fraught with all sorts of complications and uncertainties. Moreover, it involves relationships in which the lobbyists are subject to other actors who monopolize the official authority to make public decisions. Legislators, executives, and judges are all integral parts of on-going institutions and systems with their own rules and customs. Lobbyists are dependent for access, information, cooperation, and votes upon the principal actors of these systems who may themselves identify more closely with or owe their primary loyalties to their political institutions, electoral constituencies, broader constituencies, political parties, executives, their own convictions, or to other groups.

Those groups that seek to initiate new policies encounter special obstacles, for they may be compelled to operate successfully through two houses of the legislature as well as the executive, and, subsequently, they may be forced into the courts. Compromises and political adjustments, the timetables and priorities of other actors, all enter into whatever arrangements are made. If interest groups seek to intervene in the political parties and appeal to the electorate to affect the nomination and selection of candidates, they encounter other difficulties. Traditional habits of party identification and voting and the significance of the candidate's personality in American politics pose obstacles that inhibit the success of interest group involvement in the candidate selection process. In addition, the party organization may control this process. And an appeal to the party conventions for support may result in compromises that the party must make for internal unity or in order not to antagonize other groups. Many candidates run on their own platforms, moreover, ignoring that of the state or national party at their own convenience.

Both the initiative and the referendum are particularly attractive alternatives under such circumstances. The former, especially, affords interest groups an opportunity to bypass completely the legislature, parties, the executive, and often the courts, if what is proposed is a constitutional amendment. Through the referendum, authoritative decisions that have been enacted by the legislature and executive may be suspended in their operation and, subsequently, nullified without any need to persuade either the legislators or the executive to reverse themselves. Until very recently, when the judiciary agreed to rule on apportionment matters, legislators who refused to obey their constitution's mandate to reapportion could not be compelled to act. Only through the initiative, which bypassed them, could a plan of reapportionment be considered and adopted.

The initiative, as well as the referendum, may also be utilized to overrule previous legislative action—and in a binding fashion. In 1963, for example, the California legislature adopted the Rumford Act that forbade discrimination on the basis of color, race, religion, national origins, or ancestry in the rental or sale of housing. Rather than seek its repeal through a referendum, the California Real Estate Association hit upon the idea of an initiative constitutional amendment that not only would nullify this act but also prohibit future legislatures from adopting such laws. This interest group and its allies succeeded in qualifying such an initiative for the ballot. In the general election of 1964, the voters approved an initiative constitutional amendment forbidding the state, its agencies, or its subdivisions from infringing on the right of a property owner to lease, rent, or sell to anyone he chose; hotels and similar lodgings were excluded.

. In some states, the attractiveness of the initiative statute is enhanced by its invulnerability to subsequent legislative action. If the legislative initiative can only be pushed through by its sponsor, subsequent legislatures are restricted in their power to alter or to repeal it, except by extraordinary majorities. In California and in a number of other western states at different periods, legislation adopted through the initiative could not be amended or repealed by the state legislature alone. If the legislature wanted to act on such a statute, it had to be sent back to the people in the form of a referendum. In Oregon, for example, the legislature was prohibited from amending or repealing any initiative law for a two year period. The power of the Oregon legislature was expanded, in 1952, permitting it to amend initiative statutes by a two-thirds vote of each house but not to repeal such statutes.

The attractiveness of the initiative and referendum for interest groups is attested to by additional features.

(A) A SMALL FRACTION OF THE ELECTORATE CAN QUALIFY A PROPOSAL FOR THE BALLOT   All that an interest group must do to qualify a proposal for the ballot is draft a proper petition and secure a small percentage of signatures from the registered voters. In California, the minimum number of signatures for initiatives and referenda is eight per cent of those voting for the governor in the last election. Alaska requires ten per cent but Arkansas has three different requirements: eight per cent for a statutory initiative; ten per cent for an initiative constitutional amendment; six per cent for a referendum. The requirements vary among the twenty states that provide for direct legislation.

It is often easier for a group to solicit these signatures itself or to pay a professional firm for this task than to persuade the legislative committees to recommend its bill or to obtain a favorable consideration for it in the form desired by the group on the floor of both legislative chambers. Signing a petition is a much more casual act for the ordinary voter than is a vote for the legislator. Members of the electorate represent no one but themselves. They are not required to enter into the complex calculus of votes, arguments, and political considerations that confront legislators and executives. Since a signature merely helps place a measure on the ballot, citizens do not find it onerous to respond to requests that they sign. They can be appealed to, moreover, under the "fair play" argument that the people should have a chance to consider a proposal. And their signatures can be solicited anywhere, at super markets and in churches as well as by house-to-house canvassing. The difference in the ease and even in the quality of action demanded of the legislative actor and the signer in the electorate in responding to the appeal of interest groups is significant.

(B) ISSUES ARE EASILY SIMPLIFIED; THE VOTER MUST RESPOND ONLY "YES" OR "NO"   Initiatives and referenda possess a great virtue in that they are relatively simple and demand only a simple response. They are acted upon directly by members of the electorate who are not entangled in the web of relationships that envelop legislators and executives. Once a voter has indicated his choice, moreover, he is free from the responsibilities and worries of public policy considerations. Legislators must assess how a vote on any measure will affect their relations with other legislators and prospects for their own legislation. They must consider how constituents, party leaders, or interest groups will judge their actions.

That which an interest group proposes via the form of direct legislation emerges as an issue that can be simplified for mass consumption. The legislative, executive, and judicial systems magnify the complexities of issues and involve the scrutiny and judgment of experts, many of whom hold positions of public power. It is true that public debate often rages around direct legislation, thereby reintroducing the element of complexity; nevertheless, a member of the electorate votes directly on an issue, either for or against it. No recommittal motions or crippling amendments are in order.

(C) POLITICAL PARTIES CAN BE BYPASSED Candidates for public office and political parties generally avoid involving themselves in controversial issues on the ballot. Most state and local parties are not strongly issue oriented anyway. Their platforms serve more to compromise internal factions and placate powerful groups associated with them. If parties and candidates become embroiled in issues upon which the people vote directly and which are bitterly contested by opposing sets of interest groups, they risk antagonizing some of their own partisans as well as focusing upon themselves the active hostility of other supporters or opponents of these measures. With both candidates and issues on the ballot at the same time, sanctions against the former can be easily applied. Parties tend, therefore, to concern themselves principally with their candidates; and candidates, as a rule, avoid becoming entangled in initiative or referenda campaigns.

Politicians and parties do involve themselves, at times, in such campaigns; and for some, the consequences have been disastrous. The Ohio Republican Party and its state ticket were virtually blackjacked into supporting and campaigning for a "right-to-work" initiative drive which backfired. At a meeting of Republican Party leaders and their principal business allies, who customarily provided the party with its financial support, the businessmen demanded that a "right-to-work" amendment be placed on the ballot at the time of the 1958 congressional elections. Both the state party chairman and United States Senator John W. Bricker argued vehemently against this course, contending that it would endanger the entire Republican slate. Nevertheless, the business leaders prevailed over the objections of the party leaders.

Both the Republican gubernatorial and the U.S. senatorial candidates subsequently endorsed the proposed initiative amendment. Union labor, which had not particularly demonstrated any real power at the polls in Ohio, now discovered a ready-made issue with which to appeal to the voters. Even traditional, Republican rural areas reacted strongly against the "right-to-work" proposal. Not only did Senator Bricker and the Republican gubernatorial candidate go down to defeat with their initiative, which was overwhelmingly rejected, but also the Democrats captured control of both houses of the Ohio legislature. Although other issues and circumstances also affected the election, Democrats, Republicans, and neutrals alike conceded that the "right-to-work" initiative had adversely affected the Republican candidates.

That same year, in California, the Republican gubernatorial candidate, United States Senator William F. Knowland, voluntarily adopted a "right-to-work" initiative as a central issue in his campaign. The incumbent Republican governor disassociated himself from both the proposed amendment and Knowland's candidacy. The Republican governor had been elected with state AFL endorsement; its incumbent secretary-treasurer traditionally allied himself with certain Republican politicians. But with Senator Knowland running as the Republican nominee on a "right-to-work" campaign, even this Republican inclined head of the AFL was compelled to join the CIO in endorsing the Democratic candidate. Knowland's espousal of the initiative drove the two labor interest groups together, whereas previously they had been divided. The AFL leader led the campaign against the initiative, and both the Republican gubernatorial candidate and the initiative that he embraced were decisively defeated.

Other candidates and parties have, at times, intervened in direct legislation controversies but generally under very special circumstances. By 1957–58, in Oklahoma, it had become politically respectable for candidates to take a positive position on the repeal of prohibition. Nonetheless, the candidate who captured the Democratic nomination for governor in 1958 avoided a direct confrontation with the Drys. He did not personally advocate repeal, but he merely promised that, if elected, he would call a special election on a repeal proposal. In the run-off primary, even the candidate of the Dry forces was compelled to adopt this position. During the campaign, the successful candidate repeatedly assured the voters that he would take no personal part in the repeal election. On the other hand, in the 1964 California campaign on the initiative constitutional amendment to rule out antidiscrimination legislation on housing, the Republican

United States Senator, Thomas H. Kuchel, strongly opposed the proposition. However, he was not a candidate that year; and he had engaged in a bitter factional battle with certain members of his party who subsequently endorsed the initiative.

Party leaders are more likely to take sides on initiatives dealing with reapportionment because the fortunes of their parties are intimately involved in such measures, and they seem to suffer no adverse consequences thereby. Leaders of political parties may, in fact, even utilize interest groups to push initiatives on reapportionment proposals for them in order to give the campaign a nonpartisan character. In 1952, leaders of the Young Democrats and Young Republicans in Oregon came to an agreement on the desirability of securing compliance with existing constitutional provisions regarding apportionment. In order to conduct a nonpartisan campaign, they approached the League of Women Voters, who at their state convention had urged such a course. The three combined in the Non-Partisan Committee for Constitutional Reapportionment; the parties undertook to raise the necessary funds for the campaign, and the League assumed responsibility for collecting the signatures and spearheading the drive. In the reapportionment initiative campaign that the League of Women Voters sponsored and directed in the state of Washington, in 1954, the sympathetic Republican state chairman encouraged this women's group on the premise that their sponsorship would provide the measure with a non-partisan flavor.

(D) POLICY AND ADMINISTRATION CAN BE AFFECTED WITHOUT COMPROMISING INTEREST GROUP PROPOSALS   Professor Winston W. Crouch has suggested that probably the most significant reason interest groups resort to initiatives is that they desire to have their proposals adopted or defeated in the form they propose. In the legislature the proponents of a measure might have to accept a number of amendments, or even see it transformed from what was originally intended. Because the interest group drafts the legislation that will be voted upon, the intent and detailed provisions of the proposal can be preserved so that a vote is held exactly on the measure that the group wishes.

If it so desires, the interest group may draft an extremely detailed constitutional amendment, thereby ensuring the fullest protection possible for its proposal. An initiative amendment that the McLain old-age pension movement pushed through, in 1948, in California, actually went into details regarding executive personnel as well as administrative policy. By its terms, it not only removed from the governor responsibility for appointing the director of the California

Department of Social Welfare but also it removed the incumbent director. Three specific individuals were named in the amendment who were to be eligible to succeed each other as director. The first one designated was the secretary-treasurer of the interest group that had sponsored the initiative. Control of old-age assistance programs was removed from the counties and placed under the state's agency. Policy changes included the removal of relative responsibility requirements and a lowering of the eligibility requirements for old-age assistance benefits. In addition, to support the cost of the increased and liberalized old-age assistance program, a prior lien was placed on the general fund of the state. In the 1930's, an off-shoot of the Townsend Movement in Colorado, the National Annuity League, had also written into that state's constitution a similar lien on the state's treasury to guarantee liberalized old-age assistance payments.

(E) It Energizes the Interest Group   Initiative and referenda campaigns act as catalytic agents upon the membership of interest groups. A campaign on an issue of vital, direct relevance to the group supplies the members with a concrete purpose, engages them in a battle, and may even provide them with tangible, recognizable enemies against whom to fight. Although there are, of course, psychological as well as political risks involved in defeat, the campaign, itself, serves to bind members closer to their organization and their leaders. The campaign has the added attraction of cutting much less across multiple group membership lines than does involvement in contests between parties and their candidates.

Well-established groups concerned with protecting the status quo are not as a rule as much in need of such stimuli. But the leaders of marginal groups may view the campaign as serving a useful organizational function. Once the leaders of the Townsend Movement recognized the potential inherent in initiative campaigns, they sought repeatedly to qualify their initiatives. In their most ambitious campaign, involving proposals in four western states, in 1944, the Townsend leadership succeeded in reducing drastically its membership losses and actually in reversing its financial losses.

(F) Direct Legislative Campaigns May Have Long-Range Results   Not all initiatives that fail are necessarily unsuccessful. They may serve as vehicles for policy proposals that, given sufficient prominence and political support, later find their way into legislative embodiment. The political attractiveness of such proposals can influence legislators and political parties to move part way, at least, toward meeting the objectives of the interest groups. Legislators, executives, and political parties may find, that with the appropriate compromises to make the proposals more palatable, they can incorporate into their own political forces the publics in the electorate which favor these measures.

Direct Legislation Poses Its Own Problems and Disadvantages for Interest Groups

Although only a small percentage of signatures is required, collecting signatures presents an insurmountable obstacle for some groups. Even obtaining the 50,000 valid signatures which the Oregon League of Women Voters accomplished has frustrated groups more powerful than the League in that state. In 1948, the California Townsendites filed 347,000 signatures, much more than was necessary, only to discover that the initiative was disqualified because so many signatures were declared invalid. In the highly populated state of California, the number of required signatures has increased with the voting population from 205,000 in 1948 and 350,000 in 1960 to approximately 500,000 in 1964.

Accumulating the required number of valid signatures has increasingly proved so difficult that, unless interest groups possess a large dispersed membership or the finances to hire professional firms, they find it impossible to undertake successful qualification drives. On the other hand, Oregon law actually forbids any paid circulation of initiative petitions. Its interest groups are compelled either to rely upon their own organization and zeal, to compromise their proposals in order to attract the support of other groups, or to forgo such a strategy altogether.

In California, where signature collecting has become big business, a number of special firms offer their services for conducting initiative and referenda campaigns. The famous Whitaker and Baxter firm of Campaigns, Inc., made its initial reputation by providing the know-how and direction for such campaigns.[2] Frequently, they have been involved simultaneously on a number of issues at election time.

(A) Direct Legislation Campaigns Are Expensive   Professional services to obtain signatures are expensive. In 1950, approximately $100,000 was the asking price one California firm quoted as necessary to qualify an initiative. The cost had risen to between $150,000 and $200,000 by 1960. In some states, signatures must

---

[2] Robert J. Pitchell, "The Influence of Professional Campaign Management Firms in Partisan Elections in California," *Western Political Quarterly,* Vol. XI No. 2, June 1958, pp. 278–300; Stanley Kelley, Jr., *Professional Public Relations and Political Power,* The Johns Hopkins Press, Baltimore, 1956, Chapter II, "Whitaker and Baxter: Campaigns, Inc."

even be collected from a prescribed number of counties, which compounds the problems interest groups confront.

When one considers the cost of a controversial state-wide campaign, it is clear that the less affluent groups cannot easily resort to direct legislation. Campaigns to bring the issues to the attention of the voters may require recourse to billboards, television, radio, films, and newspaper advertisements. In California, Crouch has reported that, as early as 1936, more than $1,200,000 was spent on the chain store tax referendum, and, in 1939, the expenditures on a pension scheme exceeded $900,000. Over $648,000 was spent by the contending interest groups over an AFL-sponsored reapportionment initiative in California, in 1948. Even in Oklahoma, the Drys and Wets together spent over $600,000 on the 1959 fight to repeal prohibition, and both sides felt that they lacked sufficient funds to conduct an adequate campaign. Over $1,000,000 was spent by business groups alone in their successful effort, in 1949, to repeal the McLain pension law which had been enacted in California through an initiative a year earlier.

Whether or not the side with the most money to spend on collecting signatures and campaigning generally wins, as Crouch, Neuberger, and others have suggested, it is obvious that financial resources play a major role in direct legislation politics at the state level. Nevertheless, other factors also contribute to the success or failure of a campaign. A sufficient number of campaigns have been won by interest groups spending less money than their opponents, thus making such campaigns attractive to interest groups.

In Oklahoma, the Drys were unsuccessful in efforts to prevent the repeal of prohibiton, in 1959, despite the fact that they probably outspent the Wets. After his initiative victory, in 1948, it is doubtful whether McLain could have won any of his other direct legislation campaigns simply by spending more money than his business group opponents. He had become too vulnerable and isolated from the rest of the political community. Even the renowned firm, Campaigns, Inc., failed to put across an oil conservation proposition on the California ballot, in 1956, although it had a budget of $3,450,000, and it spent more than twice that of its opponents.

It should be kept in mind that collecting signatures and campaigning for direct legislation in the cities and counties of the United States usually do not involve such large sums. Moreover, an effective citizens' organization for mobilizing the electorate, the active use of the press, and the proper cultivation of important civic groups and community influcntials are also very significant factors. James Coleman has even contended that a low vote is a principal factor in the success of initiative and referenda campaigns for fluoridation. It is his hypothesis that the larger the vote in such community conflicts, the greater the percentage of participants who are basically not involved or integrated in the community and who tend to vote against fluoridation.[3]

(B) DIRECT LEGISLATION REQUIRES CAMPAIGN ORGANIZATION AND ALLIES   Controversial initiatives and referenda sponsored by interest groups stimulate opposition from other interest groups. Groups that are not yet organized may, under the pressure of an immediate threat, find the need and resources for establishing an organization and for engaging in a combative role.

In direct legislation campaigns, interest groups confront problems virtually identical with those political parties must overcome—they have to rally majorities in the electorate.[4] To accomplish this purpose, they must organize for combat, present their issue (rather than their candidate) to the public, seek out or organize allies in order to build their forces deeper and more widely among the various publics, and bring out the voters. Unlike political parties, they cannot depend upon any traditional identification and voting habits in the general electorate to aid them. Almost invariably, moreover, interest groups are neither organized to conduct their own direct election campaigns nor experienced in such a course. Lobbying in city hall, at the state legislature, or the Congress, and with executive actors is something very different from engagement in direct legislation campaigns, although by resorting to indirect lobbying interest groups acquire some relevant experience. One reason why public relations concerns have blossomed in an environment of direct legislation is that they fill a necessary role. For a fee, they provide the experience, the know-how, and even the organization.

Whether groups conduct their own campaigns or rely upon professional firms, one tactic all employ is to seek out allies. The same general principle applies here as in the legislative chambers where interest groups lobby. Allied groups help expand the initiating group's

[3] James S. Coleman, *Community Conflict,* The Free Press of Glencoe, Inc., New York, 1957, p. 19.

[4] E. E. Schattschneider, *Party Government,* Farrar and Rinehart, Inc., New York, 1942, Chapter VIII, "The Pressure Groups," denies that interest groups have to face such problems. Because of his concentration upon "pressure groups" at the national level, he misses entirely the fact that on the state and local levels of policy-making, interest groups as well as parties must often mobilize a majority when they appeal to the electorate on a proposition on the ballot. At one level of national policy-making, interest groups face a similar problem.

base of operations, contribute money, effort and other resources, associate the issue with the interests of others so that it is not stereotyped as narrow and parochial, and enable the sponsors to gain access to the members and organizational apparatus of their allies.

The McLain and the Townsend pension leaders sought unsuccessfully to break out from their political isolation in the community. Both eventually elicited some support from union labor groups, in part because the latter found themselves threatened with initiatives aimed against them. In 1944, Dr. Townsend and the president of the Arizona AFL campaigned together through four western states. The Arizona AFL endorsed the Townsend initiative, and the CIO as well as railway unions in the other states contributed money and worked for the Townsend cause. McLain also attracted some union support plus cooperation from the California Council for the Blind, which endorsed his proposals in 1952 and 1954.

Not only marginal groups seek allies. Public relations firms place great emphasis upon building other groups into the campaigns they manage. The more controversial the measure, the more well-established, respectable groups will reach out for allies. The Young Democrats and Young Republicans of Oregon were in need of a neutral group with high status in the state to lead publicly their fight for observance of the state's apportionment laws. The League of Women Voters met not only these requirements but provided a valuable mass base for collecting the specified number of signatures. Organized labor was also linked into the campaign, although not so closely as to arouse the suspicion or opposition of business groups. And with the endorsement of the Grange, the most influential farmer group in the state, the initiative attracted the rural component for victory.

Fluoridation campaigns at the local levels of city and county are extremely controversial, if only because the opponents feel so intensely on the issue that they introduce such divisive arguments as communism, compulsory medication, and health dangers to the community. Where local civic and business groups are not brought actively into the campaign, the profluoridationists are greatly handicapped. A 1952 study of a fluoridation referendum campaign in Cambridge, Massachusetts, reveals that the fluoridationists had neither organized properly nor involved in the campaign the League of Women Voters, the PTA's, and the powerful Cambridge Civic Association.[5] Their opponents prevailed at the election.

[5] Thomas F. A. Plaut, "Analysis of Voting Behavior on a Fluoridation Referendum," *Public Opinion Quarterly,* Vol. 23, No. 2, Summer, 1959, pp. 213–22.

The reverse occurred in two fluoridation campaigns, an initiative and a referendum election, sponsored by the anti-fluoridationists in Raleigh, North Carolina, in 1956 and 1957. The fluoridationists were led by the Junior Women's Club, a high status group, many of whose husbands were middle or upper executives or businessmen and against whom the charges of self-interest, communism, and dispensers of rat poison simply would not stick. It was the women who spearheaded the Citizens' Committee for Fluoridation and who elicited the support of virtually every civic club in the city. In addition, they thoroughly organized the precincts, especially those of middle and upper incomes; some of their precinct workers were active even in the poorer areas. Raleigh's experience shows that by actively involving the community leadership and by organizing and cultivating the proper electorate through a smoothly run precinct apparatus, an *ad hoc* fluoridation group can overcome the two limitations which Coleman found confronting fluoridation campaigns: The larger the turnout and the larger the city, the less likelihood that fluoridation would win in direct legislation campaigns.[6]

(C) INITIATIVES CAN BE SIDETRACKED AND REVERSED   Not only is certain legislation excluded from consideration by referenda in a number of states by constitutional prohibition or by a two-thirds vote of the legislators but also initiative petitions and legislation often face problems of nullification and repeal. In most states and local units of government that permit direct legislation, the legislative body may alter or repeal a law after it has been adopted by the popular vote. The reapportionment initiative which the League of Women Voters sponsored in the state of Washington, in 1956, was sharply revised by the legislature. The League challenged this action in the courts only to have the state supreme court rule in a five-to-four decision that the legislative act constituted an amendment, not a repeal of the initiative. A successful Townsend Club sponsored initiative to liberalize the old-age assistance program in Idaho, in 1942, was totally repealed by the next legislature.

In addition, initiatives and referenda involve technical, legal processes, and their sponsors must comply with detailed requirements. Hence, they are challenged, at times, in the courts by their opponents in an attempt to delay action on their proposals until after the election

---

[6] Coleman, *op. cit.,* p. 19. The turnout in Raleigh on the referendum and the initiative was 22 per cent and 27 per cent respectively; Coleman's data indicated fluoridation tended to be defeated when voter turnout ran above 30 per cent and to be adopted when it measured under 10 per cent. Coleman's data indicated that fluoridation is much less likely to be adopted in cities over 50,000 in population. However, Raleigh's population totalled approximately 90,000 at the time.

or in order that the proponents lose that momentum which a signature campaign may have created. In the Washington reapportionment campaign of 1956, opponents forced the initiative into the courts in an effort to have it declared invalid and to have the court enjoin the Secretary of State from certifying it on the ballot. An adverse ruling against the initiative by a lower court was reversed by the state supreme court only four days before the deadline for certifying ballot measures. This litigation virtually halted the League of Women Voters' campaign, a campaign that was resumed but twenty-four days before the election. In the politics of prohibition repeal in Oklahoma, in 1959, the Wets had to anticipate the possibility of the Drys taking their initiative to the courts and delaying it for at least a year.

Direct Legislation and National Policy-Making

No provision for the initiative—statutory or constitutional—exists at the national governmental level; nor are there petition referenda. Nevertheless, one set of participants in one sector of the economy has been permitted to participate in referenda on national public policy directly affecting them. As a result, their interest groups have had a voice in public policy through the referenda. In respect to agricultural legislation, the national government has afforded farmers working certain basic crops a direct, binding vote on whether they wish such legislation to go into effect. It should be noted, however, that these referenda are initiated by the legislature and the executive, that they pertain to one aspect of agricultural policy, and that no petition referenda are involved.

Initially, only advisory referenda were utilized.[7] In the period 1933–36, the Agricultural Adjustment Administration used such referenda to determine producers' sentiments on marketing quotas for corn, hogs, cotton, tobacco, and wheat. Only six such referenda were conducted, all of which were approved by votes of from 67.1 per cent to 95.6 per cent. Since 1938, the nature of these referenda has approximated the mandatory, binding referenda utilized in the states through which legislative bodies refer to the voters for their decision certain legislative proposals. Once the particular farmers who are qualified by their involvement with the crop under question have voted, the terms of the referenda become the law and bind all farmers engaged in producing this crop. The referenda have to be approved, however, by a vote of two thirds of all those participating.

[7] Ralph M. Goldman, "The Advisory Referendum in America," *Public Opinion Quarterly*, Vol. 14, No. 2, Summer, 1950, pp. 303–15.

As a consequence, whenever agricultural interest groups disagree fundamentally on policy, the referenda become bitter issues of controversy; for example, the vote on poundage controls for tobacco in May 1965 aroused extreme controversy in the South. If an administration strongly supports such legislation, the referenda become not only channels for interest groups to affect national policy by going to the "electorate" but they also become referenda on administration leadership and policy. Such was the case of the famous wheat referendum (on production controls) of 1963. With the Kennedy Administration squarely behind the referendum, the Secretary of Agriculture and some of his staff campaigned actively for its adoption. They were joined by the Farmers' Union and opposed by the American Farm Bureau Federation and the Republican Party leadership in the national legislature. Both sets of contending forces spent considerable time and money in organizing the constituency for the vote. The opposition prevailed; and, in the rejection of its new policy of production controls, the Administration suffered a sharp defeat.

As long as agriculture is treated in this special manner, farmer interests groups will be in a favored position *vis-à-vis* all other interest groups on the national scene. They alone campaign among voters for direct, binding decisions on national policy. At the same time, they operate in a special electorate, whereas interest groups concerned with state initiatives must appeal to the general population.[8]

[8] On other rare occasions the national government has involved itself in direct legislation, but only indirectly and relevant to state politics. The Revenue Act of 1962 was amended by the Eighty-seventh Congress to permit a deduction for contributions made to non-profit groups in Illinois and other states supporting or opposing the reorganization of the state judiciary in referenda held during the calendar year 1962. *Congressional Record,* 88:1, Vol. 109, No. 47, April 1, 1963, p. 4879. Because the amendment was limited to referenda occurring in that calendar year, Congress was asked to extend this provision to the calendar year 1963; judicial reform was being considered in Ohio and in other states.

GOVERNMENT IN THE MODERN WORLD

GENERAL EDITORS

Paul Y. Hammond   Nelson W. Polsby

This series seeks to put basic tools for understanding politics in the hands of the student. By presenting a variety of approaches to the study of political institutions, ideas, and behavior, it hopes to enlarge his awareness of our common problems, increase his ability to define and analyze them, and, perhaps, to enhance his capacity to meet and master them.

INTEREST GROUPS AND LOBBYING
By Abraham Holtzman
North Carolina State University

Numerous case studies and original research form the basis for this treatment of the organization and tactics of interest groups in America, with comparative glimpses at interest groups in the British and Italian political systems. Explored are various ways in which groups seek to promote policies they favor — through the executive, legislative, and judicial branches of government, and directly through the initiative and referendum. The author synthesizes contemporary interest group theory, taking into account factors relating group skills, resources, and strategies to internal and external demands upon groups and the problems and opportunities created by the political environment.

THE MACMILLAN COMPANY, 60 Fifth Avenue, New York 10011

35687